MASTER THE ENTREPRENEURIAL MINDSET

❦

BUILD THE LIFE YOU WANT, ON YOUR TERMS

CAMERON BANKS

MASTER THE ENTREPRENEURIAL MINDSET

CAMERON BANKS

ISBN: 978-1-968418-83-0

INTRODUCTION

In a world where the pace of change has accelerated dramati-cally, the entrepreneurial mindset is not just a desirable trait—it's a necessity. This book offers a transformative guide for anyone looking to harness this mindset to architect a life de-fined by personal goals and values rather than external circum-stances. It begins by exploring the profound impact of self-belief and the ability to overcome self-doubt, two critical ele-ments that often determine the trajectory of entrepreneurial success. Through relatable stories and real-world examples, readers are invited to confront and dismantle the common barriers of fear and uncertainty that stifle creativity and action.

The narrative advances by laying out a clear promise: practical, actionable frameworks that empower readers to sculpt their desired lives. These frameworks are designed to be accessible and relevant, regardless of one's background or current situa-tion, ensuring that the entrepreneurial mindset is within reach for all. The book delves into the psychological roots of com-mon entrepreneurial hurdles—fear of failure, imposter syn-drome, and the overwhelming flood of conflicting advice offering tools to transform these challenges into stepping stones.

Readers are equipped with modern strategies that are as diverse as they are practical, from mindset rewiring and resilience building to decision-making under uncertainty and creative problem-solving. Each chapter is packed with step-by-step frameworks, self-assessment tools, and real stories from founders, making the principles immediately applicable. The emphasis on actionable tools ensures that readers can move from intention to action, building confidence and resilience along the way.

Moreover, the book showcases the depth of research and credibility behind its advice, drawing insights from best-selling titles, interviews, and real-world case studies. It sets clear ex-pectations for transformation, inviting readers to engage fully and build not only a business but a life that aligns with their deepest aspirations. As readers are encouraged to dive into the chapters, they are also challenged to commit to mastering the entrepreneurial mindset, armed with the knowledge that this journey is as much about personal growth as it is about pro-fessional success.

CONTENTS

CHAPTER 1

REWIRING YOUR MINDSET FOR ENTRE-PRENEURIAL ACTION

Diagnosing Your Current Mindset

In entrepreneurship, it is important to know what state of mind one is in at that particular time in order to succeed. This self-reflective exercise includes a careful analysis of individual beliefs, attitudes, and willingness to undertake the entrepre-neurial path. The first stage in this exploration is the self-assessment, which serves as a mirror that gives a reflection on the internal scenery with regard to entrepreneurship.

This self-assessment is not a superficial look at the potential but a plunge into the heart and soul of what is deeply held by the individual and guides decision-making and action-taking. It is a diagnostic quiz, which is created to trace out the beliefs of a person, his/her risk tolerance, and action orientation. Through participation in this quiz, one can gain a better under-standing of where one lies on the spectrum of entrepreneurial readiness. The quiz is also meant to be self-disclosing and formative, an insight into areas of strength and areas that re-quire building up.

An important instrument in this process is the so-called Mindset Radar, a graphic representation of this process that helps the individual to self-score in five dimensions. The tool assists in measuring the intangible concepts of mindset into measurable aspects, to provide a clear picture of where one is good and where one should improve. The radar not only shows the strengths but also shows the blind spots that might be retarding entrepreneurial efforts.

After the assessment, one is advised to reflect critically on their results and relate them to standard entrepreneurial archetypes. These personas are archetypes, including The Planner, The Dreamer, The Reluctant Doer, and The Lone Wolf, and a number of these archetypes are the personas that most entre-preneurs may relate to. Both of the archetypes have their bene-fits and their issues, and they help one realize his or her natural tendencies and how they may influence the path of entrepre-neurship.

A very important aspect of this diagnostic phase is reflection. People are brought to mind some of the recent risks that they have managed to avoid and investigate the causes of these decisions. This reflection will be useful in establishing patterns of behavior that might be nonproductive to the success of an entrepreneur. Knowing these patterns will allow people to start making conscious moves to change their attitude to more productive and fearless action.

In addition, it is advisable to set up a personal Mindset Base-line. This baseline serves as an individual reference that may be examined back in the days and days to measure growth and change. It is a living document and strives to develop with the individual as they continue in their career as an entrepreneur, and this gives them a constant feedback loop in the develop-ment.

The process of analyzing the state of mind is not only about determining what can not be done, but also about understand-ing and glorifying the special talents that can be used to suc-ceed in entrepreneurship. By learning and accepting their pre-sent way of thinking, people are in better positions to make informed choices, take risks, and, in the end, be able to wade through the waters of entrepreneurship with a sense of confi-dence and strength.

Myth Busting: Overcoming Imposter Syndrome

The notion that only a few are meant to succeed usually domi-nates in the world of entrepreneurship, and this further pro-motes the myth that only the chosen few have an inborn en-trepreneurial character. This is a myth that can also be debilitat-ing, particularly when it is combined with the sense of impos-tor syndrome that can be so widespread, a psychological phe-nomenon in which people lack confidence in their achieve-ments and worry that they may be uncovered as a so-called fraud. Such an attitude is typical of business people, especially entrepreneurs who are usually pressured and expected to be successful.

Data and studies prove that people who become successful entrepreneurs are of varying backgrounds, and thus, there is no single road to success. The age, education, and ethnicity among the founders are diverse, which explains that entrepre-neurship does not allow one group to be more successful than another. In presenting stories of entrepreneurs with non-business or underrepresented backgrounds, we can get an understanding of how they have managed to triumph within the world of entrepreneurship, further shattering the myth that entrepreneurship is a pre-determined route.

The causes of imposter syndrome run deep in the psyche and are therefore usually triggered by early life experiences and societal expectations. This intrapersonally held self-doubt comes in the form of the so-called imposter scripts. These typical self-talk messages negatively affect self-confidence and keep the self-doubt process going. Identifying these scripts is the initial step on the road to defeating them. Entrepreneurs should start to break the false stories that keep them back by determining the causes of these thoughts.

In an effort to deal with imposter syndrome, one can utilize practical and scientifically supported strategies to reframe self-doubt and celebrate the uniqueness of being an entrepreneur. A good way of doing this is to keep a daily evidence log, and the entrepreneurs record micro-wins and progress, strength-ening their capabilities and success throughout time. This is an activity that assists in developing a portfolio of success, how-ever small, that can be relied on when the need arises.

The other effective instrument is the "Rewriting Your Founder Story" worksheet, which asks the entrepreneur to rewrite his or her story by emphasizing strengths and achievements. In being active in the creation of the narrative, they will be in a position to view themselves as the competent leaders they are and not as the impostors they believe they are.

As well, a troubleshooting guide on how to overcome impost-er feelings in typical entrepreneurial situations can be invalua-ble. In a pitch in a meeting, making connections with more advanced founders or rolling out a product with minimal ex-ternal validation, a set of strategies to rely on can give confi-dence and lower anxiety.

Finally, the way to overcome imposter syndrome is by chang-ing the mindset. It involves understanding that self-doubt is an inherent aspect of the entrepreneurial process and not a disqualifier of his or her capacity to achieve. Entrepreneurs can embrace their potential and succeed by confronting the myths that continue to validate the imposter syndrome and taking practical steps to gain confidence. The route to mastering the entrepreneurial mindset does not involve eliminating doubt but instead turning it into an engine of development and in-novation.

From Fear to Fuel: Transforming Fear of Failure

Fear of failure in the world of entrepreneurship is a big shad-ow that casts its shade over ambitions and strategies. This fear is not to be an obstacle, nonetheless. Rather, it could be used as a strong driving force and source of innovation and devel-opment. The first step to transformation is identifying what exactly scares the potential entrepreneurs. Such fears usually entail the loss of money, social humiliation, and time, all of which are potent foes in the path to becoming an entrepre-neur.

One of the effective methods of overcoming these fears is an effective technique known as Risk Rehearsal; this is a practical procedure that has been specifically created to eradicate indi-vidual anxieties of entrepreneurs. Entrepreneurs can use a contingency plan, and if X happens, then they will do Y to prepare for the worst-case scenario and make fear a normal part of their strategy. This method not only equips them with worst-case scenarios but also gives them the ability to make firm decisions when they are in the unknown.

Additional reframing of failure as a simple fact, instead of a conclusive one, promotes a healthier view of failures. This is the picture that is frequently provided by the modern founder stories when the failure of product launches is not regarded as a setback but as a possibility to turn around and become in-novative. Such a change of mind is essential, which can trans-form the supposedly crippling fear into a stepping block to success in the future.

Formal Failure Debriefing with reflection prompts will help to draw quality lessons out of every setback. This ritual motivates business people to tear down failures, learn what has gone wrong, and use the lessons to give them a new venture. In the process, they will not only learn from their errors but also gain resilience, an essential element in long-term success.

Besides, the philosophy of Fail Fast, which is contrasted with risk-taking, promotes immediate repetition and learning. The entrepreneurs may analytically evaluate what they have done, what they have not done, and what they can do next by insti-tuting a low-friction personal debrief system. This will create a culture of not being afraid of failure but being able to expect it as an essential component of learning.

By disseminating such debriefs to peers or accountability part-ners, these setbacks are further normalized, making them learning experiences. Such openness and a mutual learning culture not only reduce the fear of failure but also empower the entrepreneurial community in general.

To sum up, the path to fuel is a long trip that entails a com-plete change of perception. Learning to accept failures as a natural and informative experience as a part of the entrepre-neurship process, people can overpower their fears and direct them as the sources of innovation and success. Such an atti-tude not only equips them with the inevitable challenges of entrepreneurship but also makes them stronger and more resilient with every effort.

The Fail Fast Ritual

Failing fast stands out as the critical philosophy in the human race of entrepreneurship. This method does not urge one to take up risks without thinking, but allows the process of learn-ing from failures to happen quickly and efficiently. The spirit of failing fast is the possibility to quickly go through cycles and change the approach depending on the input and information received as a result of failure.

The core of this philosophy is the development of a personal debrief system, a system of analysis of what has gone wrong, what has worked, and what may be improved. In this system, the process is to establish a low-friction routine so that the entrepreneurs can look back at their experiences and pull valu-able insights. This kind of debrief system can be used as a tool of continuous improvement, and every failure is not regarded as a failure but as a stepping stone towards success.

It starts by understanding the difference between a failure re-sulting from a lack of diligence and a failure resulting from being careless. Failing fast is a premeditated technique in which risks are estimated and the likelihood to learn is optimized. Conversely, the failure of care is characterized by the absence of planning and anticipation, which in most instances leads to preventable mistakes. The ability to differentiate between the two would enable the entrepreneurs to undertake their busi-nesses with a growth/learning mindset.

In order to provide the fail-fast ritual, it is also important to develop a template that is to be followed during the debrief process. Some of the important elements that need to be cap-tured in this template are what went well during the undertak-ing, what did not work, and what could be done differently in the future. With the systematic approach to these areas, entre-preneurs can work out a complex image of their failures and turn it into practical insights.

Failure data is also part of this ritual that helps to make future decisions better. Through failure analysis, business people will be able to determine patterns and trends that could influence future ventures. This scientific methodology guarantees that every development phase is more knowledgeable and coordi-nated with the final objectives of the business.

Also, disclosure of these debriefs to peers or accountability partners may also improve learning. By talking to others about the failures, one normalizes the experience and is likely to gain collective learning and support. Such a group element of the fail-fast ritual creates an open and strong culture in which fail-ure is perceived as a chance to learn, not as a failure.

To make these discussions easier, entrepreneurs may introduce a "Failure Share" circle, during which people meet in order to talk about their debriefs and exchange their knowledge. The practice promotes transparency and teamwork and builds an atmosphere where learning through failure is glorified and used to achieve success later.

Finally, the fail-fast ritual does pertain to the acceptance of failure as part of the entrepreneurial process. It is a promise to study and grow, in which every failure is not the end, but a very important part of the success story. With the help of structured debriefing, data-driven learning, and collaborative learning, entrepreneurs can use the power of failure to inno-vate and succeed.

CHAPTER 2

TURNING IDEAS INTO ACTION

The Brainstorm-to-Launch Pipeline

Bringing a raw idea into life as a real product or service is a complex process requiring a planned procedure to go through the stages of development to the actual implementation. This starts with an action-oriented system of capturing and priori-tizing ideas so that only the best ideas are chosen to develop. The nature of this phase is action mapping, which is a strategic activity aimed at helping busy people simplify their creative activities.

Within action mapping, the ideas are broken down into their major elements: what impact each idea may create, how simple it can be implemented, and what steps it will take to make it a reality. Such a logical division enables a clear prioritization of the work, which is a roadmap of the brainstorming phase to the first execution milestone. Through mapping this trip, en-trepreneurs will be able to identify possible points of bottle-necks and modify their plans to change that.

One of the essentials of this pipeline is the application of an MVP (Minimum Viable Product) mindset. This strategy pro-motes fast prototyping so that the entrepreneur can put their ideas into practice and not be paralyzed by the fear of perfec-tion. The MVP is based on determining the absolute core value of an idea and eliminating non-essential features. This lean model will not only speed the launch cycle but also enable faster feedback loops that are critical to iterative improvement.

To present the point, a case of the introduction of a remote productivity device may be used as an example. To kick start this project, the project would start with a whiteboard session to identify the major functionalities, and then a user test would be used to authenticate these features. The entrepreneur can prioritize the goal and schedule their tasks by dividing them into small, manageable steps, which will help him/her to cope even during the busiest times. The task is structured so that one task is to be completed within a given limited time frame, i.e., a 15-minute action breakdown, so that progress is concur-rent and quantifiable.

A Kanban-style board or a Trello template cannot be neglect-ed in this pipeline. These tools offer a graphical guide to how the ideas may be tracked and where the momentum could be lost. Through visual record keeping, the entrepreneur is guar-anteed to keep all the team members and the project on track, as it is being brainstormed right up to launch.

Also, one cannot overestimate the significance of feedback. Early user feedback is also essential to perfecting the MVP and making sure that the product fulfills the needs of the market. This feedback cycle is enabled by prompt actions and scripts that are meant to confront the first users with constructive criticism. Integrating these practices in the pipeline, entrepre-neurs are able to make informed decisions so that the product fits better in the market.

Finally, the Brainstorm-to-Launch Pipeline is concerned with turning abstract ideas into an action plan. It demands a crea-tive and organized balance, allowing entrepreneurs to find their way through the intricacies of product development with com-fort and speed. Through such a systematic process, the entre-preneurs can reduce risks, allocate resources better, and hasten the process of taking the idea to a market-ready product.

MVP Mindset: Rapid Prototyping

Within the entrepreneurship community, there is a concept known as a Minimum Viable Product (MVP) that can be es-sential to anyone keen to test their concepts without falling into the trap of perfection. The MVP philosophy is concerned with getting down to the basics of what you are trying to cre-ate- what really matters to it, and removing the unnecessary clutter that will only postpone implementation. This not only saves time and resources but also enables quick iterations, which rely on feedback that can be obtained in the real world.

The MVP philosophy recommends the quick launch and learning phase as opposed to months spent on building a product only to realise that the market has changed or that the product is not appealing to the users. This helps you to test assumptions and collect insights faster by determining the absolute core value of your idea and then making a simplified version of your idea to deliver such value.

It starts with what should be contained in the MVP. Here is a process of differentiating between must-have features and those that are just nice-to-have. A good exercise is to find out what the 30-minute version of my product is. In answering this, you will have an opportunity to concentrate on providing the core of your idea without being burdened by extravagant features that might not be of much essence at the initial stages.

There are many real-life examples of entrepreneurs who have been able to make use of the MVP mindset successfully. Take the example of a founder who tested their idea during a week-end with the help of basic tools such as Carrd and Stripe. A simple landing page and email collection helped to determine interest and collect feedback without a huge investment. Not only was this approach risk-reducing, but it also gave invalua-ble insights that were used in future development.

Entrepreneurs are advised to use no-code and low-code tools to help them rapidly create a prototype. Through these plat-forms, non-technical founders can build operating prototypes without knowing a lot of coding. It focuses on speed and rapidity, and enables entrepreneurs to pivot fast on the basis of user feedback.

There is also the MVP culture of feedback. MVP is not a final stage but the first stage of the process of continuous im-provement. Interviewing the early users as part of a structured feedback exercise will give invaluable insights into how the product can be developed further. An outreach script could be as simple as asking users what they liked, what they didn't like, and what they would improve.

Practically, MVP might be designed as a 48-hour sprint, during which entrepreneurs will spend a weekend bringing an idea to life. This time-boxed process encourages focus and urgency, essential traits for any startup. The sprint starts on Friday evening with brainstorming, continues on Saturday, tests on Sunday afternoon, and launches on Sunday. This is a disci-plined approach to make sure that ideas are not only con-ceived but also implemented.

Finally, an MVP orientation is a philosophy regarding busi-ness. It demands having the ability to embrace imperfection and perceive failure as a learning experience, not as a failure. Through prioritizing rapid prototyping, entrepreneurs are able to test their ideas more effectively, save time in marketing, and have a higher probability of success in a competitive environ-ment.

The 48-Hour Side Hustle Sprint

When applied to a simple idea and followed through to a physical product or service, it can take a structured, time-boxed process only a weekend. The sprint method is supposed to fit the hectic timetable of those who aspire to become entrepre-neurs and motivate them to devote all their energies to devel-oping the minimum viable version of their side hustle. It starts with a definite plan, and the weekend is divided into managea-ble parts, which are focused on action rather than perfection.

On Friday evening, the sprint begins with a brainstorming session. This is a very important first step, because it precon-ditions all that comes after. The participants are invited to be inspired by their personal experiences, market gaps, or new trends. The objective is to come up with a short list of ideas that can be generated quickly using the available resources. The participants can also avoid the pitfall of overcomplicating their original idea because it would be simpler and more viable to adhere to simplicity and practicality first.

Saturday is given to construction work. The current stage is characterized by the focus on fast development based on no-code or low-code frameworks, supporting rapid progression without involving deep technical skills. Applications such as Trello or Airtable may prove priceless when planning the work and monitoring progress. The emphasis is placed on the crea-tion of a prototype that will embody the spirit of the idea, but not an immaculate result.

Saturday afternoon is concerned with testing and iteration. This will entail establishing a feedback loop involving a small circle of potential users or peers who can give actionable feed-back in an instant. Students will be advised to accept construc-tive criticism, which will be used to improve what is being offered. This is a critical phase of detecting any significant defects or improvement points before the actual launch.

Sunday is all about start-ups. The idea is to launch the product or service to more people, although it may not be in excellent condition. This is because, in addition to testing the response of the market, it creates momentum and confidence among the participants. Even a successful minor launch can give im-petus and confirmation to further development, which is re-quired after the first sprint.

In the process, participants should monitor typical roadblocks, including technology problems, self-doubt, or scope creep. Facts are given to overcome these problems, so that im-provements are not made because of the unexpected difficul-ties.

At the conclusion of the weekend, the participants will have gone through the entire lifecycle of a product launch, starting with its conception and its release to the people. This sprint not only trains them to be able to do things fast, but it also imparts an attitude of action and strength. The 48-hour chal-lenge is a strong reminder that one can achieve a lot in a very limited time when they are focused and determined to do so, which preconditions further entrepreneurial activity.

Beating Analysis Paralysis

The issue of making less-than-perfect information decisions at the juncture of entrepreneurship can easily stall the process. One of the measures that can be used to overcome this stag-nation is a practical strategy of using a decision matrix, in which it is easy to undertake a step without having to analyze it in depth. The decision grid is designed in the form of a 2x2 grid where potential actions are classified based on their ef-fects and effort. The approach is clean, as it gives a pictorial representation of options that balance possible gains against the resources needed.

Take the case of an entrepreneur who is in a dilemma on whether to start a webinar or an ebook. The matrix assists in the consideration of which choice needs less effort and yields a larger impact. Plotting these choices, one will see where to put their direct attention, make a leap, and avoid the trap of over-researching and endless comparisons. This is also an effective tool in pointing out the pitfalls of analysis paralysis, which can be a serious obstacle when the fear of making the wrong choice paralyzes any decision.

In order to successfully apply this type of matrix, one should start with a list of all possible options. The options are then rated on the basis of their possible impact and the effort re-quired. This is aimed at finding the decision that has the great-est impact and least effort, and that gives a definite way ahead. This approach promotes the use of good enough decisions to be made very fast, as opposed to having a perfect solution, which may never happen.

This matrix is not only a decision-making tool, but is an action catalyst. It contains a printable template and examples of real-life situations, e.g., what feature of the product to test first. Through this matrix, entrepreneurs can make sound decisions within the shortest time possible and hence keep up in their businesses.

Along with the decision matrix, the chapter focuses on the pitfalls of over-research to avoid. The unending comparison and data retrieval may cause paralysis and then opportunities lost. Instead, it is about calculated risks and learning from the results, and not trying to be perfect in all decisions.

The decision matrix is also a learning and reflection tool. Mak-ing decisions again and comparing the consequences would enable entrepreneurs to optimise their decision-making and better understand what can be called a good enough decision. The regular learning process will be instrumental in the devel-opment of confidence and resilience amid the hectic atmos-phere of entrepreneurship.

Finally, the chapter proposes a change of mindset, whereby it should not be about perfect information but about taking action with the information at hand. It is a proactive strategy aimed at empowering the entrepreneurs so that they can go through this uncertainty with more ease and confidence. Through the decision matrix, any entrepreneur must move towards progress rather than perfection, a scenario that en-courages a culture of constant learning and reinvention.

CHAPTER 3

BUILDING AND LEADING ENTREPRE-NEURIAL TEAMS

Recruiting for Mindset

Even in the field of entrepreneurship, where innovation and flexibility are the most important, with recruiting, the art goes well beyond the limits of conventional requirements and re-sumes. The attention is drawn to the people who may be de-scribed as possessing a specific kind of mentality, that is, hav-ing a growth orientation, being action-oriented, resilient, and having an unquenchable inquisitiveness. That spirit is the foundation of entrepreneurial achievement, and teams can balance the unpredictable waters of innovation with flexibility and courage.

The recruitment process starts with a radical change of the outlook, in that the focus would be on finding the potential and not merely reviewing the past performance. This comes in the form of a recruitment philosophy that places a greater emphasis on entrepreneurial qualities, understanding that tech-nical ability and educational background, though important, are not always an indicator of how a person will perform in a fast-paced, start-up culture.

An essential part of this plan is the introduction of behavioral interview questions, which are to be used to extract the entre-preneurial potential. Examples include candidates may be re-quired to narrate a situation where they were required to take decisive action with incomplete information or when there was an unexpected project failure. These questions are not only about the answers but also about the exposure of candidate thoughts, adaptation, and learning.

Besides, assessment tasks and trial projects are priceless assets in this process. Employers may also be in a position to test the first-hand approach of potential employees in solving real-life challenges by creating situations that necessitate the candi-dates to exhibit ownership, adaptability, and creativity. An as-signment such as a 48-hour challenge can look into the capa-bility of a candidate to perform under pressure, and peer feedback from the collaborators of the trial can help to pro-vide further insights into their collaborative and leadership skills.

In order to augment these tests, a scoring rubric would be necessary to assess candidates on mindset cues and not cre-dentials alone. Action bias, comfort with ambiguity, and the capability to learn through feedback should be the key catego-ries in this rubric. This makes sure that the evaluation process is in line with the entrepreneurial values that the organization wishes to develop.

The final objective is to have a team that is not only equipped with the skills required but also has a team spirit of entrepre-neurship. This spirit plays a critical role in breeding an owner-ship culture in the organization, where members of the team are enabled to behave like founders, take initiative, and lead innovation internally.

Traditional command-and-control models are replaced in this environment with decentralized, founder-oriented models that are decentralized in autonomy and accountability. This can be made clear with practical systems like a Decision Rights Matrix, and weekly ownership check-ins can keep the team on track and keep them motivated. Rituals and recognition systems of rewarding founder-like behavior further instill this culture in the team members, making them adopt and internalize the entrepreneurial mindset as part of their professional identity.

Mindset recruiting is more than a simple approach to hiring; it is a core part of developing strong, creative teams that will be able to survive in the current environment of entrepreneur-ship. Focusing on mindset rather than on the resume, organi-zations will be able to achieve the maximum potential of their teams, leading to consistent growth and innovation in the constantly changing world.

The Ownership Culture Blueprint

Ownership culture is a revolutionary aspect of organizations, and it changes the paradigm of common command systems to a place where autonomy and accountability are encouraged. This cultural change is not only the decentralization of deci-sions, but the ability of every team member to think and act as a founder. The culture is critical to improving team perfor-mance, retention, and innovation.

A clear opposition to the traditional command-and-control models is placed at the center of the ownership culture. Hier-archical decision-making is a typical feature of traditional mod-els in which the directives are issued at the top and the deci-sions of the people on the ground are restricted. Conversely, an ownership culture promotes a founder-driven model in which there is a decentralization of decision rights to the team. This model not only enhances accountability but also makes sure that decisions are made by those who are closest to the information and context at hand.

This culture is to be implemented by coming up with practical systems that spread autonomy within the organization. One such tool is the Decision Rights Matrix, which makes it very clear who makes what decision. This is the blueprint of ac-countability because everyone understands the roles and has the mandate to perform within his or her area. This clarity can be maintained through regular ownership check-ins in which teams can keep track of goals and responsibilities.

Leadership is vital in the process of expectation setting and fostering self-management. This model requires leaders to give a framework and resources to the teams and then step aside to enable them to prosper. The potential of this approach can be seen in real-life examples of a team member who suggests and spearheads a new product feature on his own. These needs need to be promoted and approved, and the im-portance of the individual contribution to the bigger organiza-tional objectives emphasized.

The ownership culture can only be maintained with recogni-tion systems. Founder-like behaviors should also be rewarded, and not only results. Awards such as the Founder mindset can be given monthly to those with the entrepreneurial spirit, and this will make them feel a sense of pride and encouragement in the team. This culture is further instilled through peer-nominated recognition ceremonies, whereby teams are able to share in group success as well as individual contributions.

This culture can also be strengthened by turning ordinary meetings into experiment-first meetings. Meeting by experi-ment and hypothesis, respectively, teams can transition to action-oriented and dynamic discussions, as opposed to status updates. This methodology promotes team members to rapid-ly experiment with ideas, gaining experience and improving on them through learning, creating an atmosphere of constant improvement.

The ownership culture also depends on feedback mecha-nisms. Peer review rituals, e.g., Feedback Fridays, may help demystify feedback and promote a growth mindset. The ritu-als are meant to be low-friction and action learning with the aim of developing a safe environment, where honest and con-structive interactions can take place to spur personal and pro-fessional development.

Finally, the culture blueprint ownership is that of building a culture in which all the team members are given the empow-erment to behave as founders. It involves a desire to divide the decision-making process, acknowledge personal contribu-tions, and create an endless learning process. Organizations can unleash their potential by implementing these principles and become the source of innovation and success.

Meeting Makeovers

In the hectic entrepreneurial environment, meetings tend to be associated with routine, and they are deprived of their potential as a potent driver of innovation and development. Replacing the usual meeting format with lively, experiment-based ses-sions is a disruptive solution for the team that aims to be agile and impactful. Meetings can be transformed into a source of creativity and practical revelations by changing the emphasis of the status updates to hypothesis-based discussions.

This change is in its essence a transformation to an experi-ment-first structure, in which every gathering agenda is thor-oughly designed around a set of hypotheses or tests. Rather than recapping on what has been done, the participants are encouraged to present ready to test ideas. This not only puts the focus of the meeting in sharpshooting but also aligns the team to shared goals, creating a culture of constant experimen-tation and learning.

A planned agenda is key to carrying this through. The meet-ings must start with clearly stated hypotheses that the team will be exploring. As an example, a product team may provide a hypothesis, such as, "Should we change the pricing model, the level of user engagement will rise by 20 percent? The agenda must then outline the measures of success and draw the plan for the further steps to be taken to test these ideas. Such a format makes sure that any debate is purpose-based and geared to achieving practical results.

Facilitation is very important in making these sessions work. Objectivity and inclusivity can be supported through rotating facilitators so that no one single opinion gets the upper hand in the discussion. Silent brainstorming and digital whiteboard-ing are the techniques that may democratize participation, and everyone can be heard without discrimination. Such inclusivity does not just add variety to the discussion but also digs up a wide range of ideas and solutions.

Strong follow-up guidelines should be entrenched to ensure the momentum is maintained outside the meeting room. Ac-tion checklists and online applications such as Slack reminder bots may be utilized to monitor the course of experiments and accountability. With a consistent review and reiteration of these experiments, the teams can seize the pertinent lessons, refine their tactics, and generate continuous enhancement.

Finally, the reorganization of meetings to focus on experimen-tation instead of fixed reporting turns them into critical growth and innovation chances. Teams can be nimble and confident in the face of the complexity of the entrepreneurship world by establishing an environment of collaboration in which hy-pothesizing and learning take precedence. It also improves productivity and instills a mentality of adaptation and resili-ence, which are the only two qualities that can be utilized to survive in the ever-changing business environment.

Feedback as Fuel

When taken constructively, feedback is not a simple critique, and it can instead be an intensifier of change. It is the throb of any successful entrepreneurial ecosystem, and it acts as a mir-ror, a reflection of the truth of what one is doing and what strategies one is going to use. The nature of feedback does not concern the delivery but the reception and application of the feedback. When entrepreneurship taps into feedback power-fully, it is possible to move through the difficulties of business in a more nimble and discerning way.

The initial move toward using feedback constructively is to develop a culture in which it is perceived as an opportunity and not a threat. An atmosphere in which feedback is regularly given and appreciated can be used to develop trust and open-ness. This includes the creation of rituals to make feedback normal, like Feedback Fridays, on which team members are invited to provide constructive feedback systematically. These rituals make feedback less mystical and more of a participatory growth instrument.

The feedback process can also be improved greatly through the implementation of peer review rituals. These rituals must be made low-friction and actionable, e.g., the Stop/Start/Continue format, whereby people can easily con-vey what should be stopped, started, or continued. These pro-cesses can be supported with the help of digital tools such as Slack integrations or Google Forms, and allow feedback to be easily accessible and managed. This is aimed at streamlining the feedback procedure to make it efficient and effective.

The most important aspect in feedback exchanges is psycho-logical safety. Clear rules of engagement need to be set by the teams that foster honesty and constructiveness. This consists of establishing norms that hinder defensive responses and promote free discussions. Teams can improve their learning and development processes by learning to avoid pitfalls of feedback, including transforming ambiguous criticism into actionable steps.

Besides, feedback is concerned with determining not only what went wrong but also what went right. It is a process that involves the celebration of failures and wins. Recognizing and considering productive failures would help to instill in the teams the culture of learning through errors. This would make the difference between being faulty and having a more bal-anced perspective that values progress and learning.

Finally, feedback is a kind of self-improving loop, an evolving mechanism that promotes sustainability and creativity. The entrepreneur can integrate feedback into the organisational culture to make it a solid growth engine. The issue is to con-vert feedback into an action plan and not just a report that remains at rest.

Finally, when utilized properly, feedback is also a potent force that makes entrepreneurs successful. It will need a change of attitude whereby feedback is not the end but the beginning of new ideas and plans. It is this ability to convert feedback into fuel that makes a successful entrepreneur stand out against others. This adaptability, growth, and listening capacity are what end up guiding the path of entrepreneurial enterprises to be resilient and competitive even in a constantly changing business environment.

CHAPTER 4

NAVIGATING THE ENTREPRENEURIAL ECOSYSTEM

The Micro-Mastermind Model

In the dynamic landscape of entrepreneurship, where chal-lenges and uncertainties are constants, the concept of a micro-mastermind group emerges as a beacon of support and growth. This model is particularly advantageous for entrepre-neurs at all stages, offering a structured yet flexible environ-ment that fosters mutual accountability. Within the ever-changing environment of entrepreneurship, when things be-come difficult and uncertain, the notion of a micro-mastermind group becomes a ray of hope and development. Such a model proves especially beneficial to entrepreneurs at any of the levels, as it provides a highly organized and flexible space that promotes a sense of collective responsibility, shar-ing of ideas, and emotional investment. Micro-mastermind groups, unlike the large mastermind events or traditional net-working, are small groups that are more focused on depth than breadth, where every member of the group receives per-sonalized attention and feedback.

What makes a micro-mastermind group so effective is that it provides a safe environment in which businesspeople can openly discuss their successes and challenges and use the col-lective knowledge of the group to find their own path. Such a peer-based resilience circle is not only a source of emotional support but also a potent means of long-term development, as it can assist its members in being resilient when faced with adversity.

The creation of a micro-mastermind group is achieved through the identification of potential members with comple-mentary skills and objectives. This is a very important step in selection since the synergy in the group can be very important in influencing how effective the group becomes. The optimal group size is normally three to five individuals, which gives the chance of different points of view, yet it is a small group that facilitates free discussion.

After creating the group, the second thing is to map the struc-ture and best practices in meetings. Good meetings are nor-mally opened with a well-laid-out agenda that addresses wins, sharing, roadblocks, and promises. Rituals which include: hot seat rotation, where a single member is given the attention and feedback of the group, and Idea jam, a group brainstorming session, are part of ensuring that the group is kept engaged and that every session is fruitful.

The ground rules and the group charter should be established in order to maintain engagement and maximize the value of the group, which provides the expectation of how to partici-pate and maintain confidentiality. Such a pillar of trust leads to the members being vulnerable and honest, creating a culture of shared growth and responsibility.

Such challenges as scheduling clashes or member dropouts are inescapable. Still, they can be addressed with the help of such techniques as periodically changing the facilitator and keeping the meeting schedules flexible. The effectiveness and longevity of the group are dependent on the adaptation and evolution of the group to meet the needs of its members.

Essentially, the micro-mastermind model is not just a support system, but a strategic system that enables entrepreneurs to tap the power of collective intelligence. Through the creation of an environment of trust and mutual respect, these groups allow their members to pursue new ideas and challenges directly and, eventually, realize their entrepreneurial goals. The close contact and experience help members gain a better insight into their strengths and weaknesses, which leads to both personal and professional development.

This model serves as a testament to the power of community in entrepreneurship, highlighting that even in the most solitary of pursuits, success is often a collaborative effort. By embrac-ing the micro-mastermind model, entrepreneurs can build a robust support system that not only propels them forward but also enriches their journey with shared wisdom and camarade-rie.

Finding Allies in Unlikely Places

Success in the great arena of entrepreneurship can depend not just on the capabilities one has but equally on the quality and the multiculturality of his or her network. Think of the un-tapped potential in the non-traditional networks- those secre-tive allies who lie outside the standard business networks. Such allies could be as diverse as an alum network, local community groups, or even hobby clubs. When the definition of what a network is is expanded, it opens up a treasure fund of re-sources and assistance, which would have otherwise been under wraps.

Let's consider an example of an entrepreneur who finds a key partner in a local bike club. This person, at first merely some-one on the weekend ride on a bike, happens to be a priceless beta-user of a new application. Similarly, envision a founder who partners with a local artist, not through a deliberate busi-ness connection, but through a community art class. Their collaboration reinvigorates the branding of their startup, with the intensive effect of such a seemingly fortuitous meeting.

The trick to exploiting these improbable alliances is the capaci-ty to map out the secret network. This means determining and contacting friends, family, former peers, and even service pro-viders who could have contacts or knowledge about your tar-get industry. Making this network is a procedure that can be methodical and purposeful. With the help of such resources as a "Hidden Network

Worksheet," one can start assembling the puzzle of potential allies that encompass them.

Upon the identification of these connections, the activation process is the next step. This takes some form of confidence and outreach strategy. In this respect, the simple scripts and templates might be priceless and offer a pattern of re-establishing communication with people and initiating mean-ingful dialogue. It can be a short text to a long-time friend or a more formal email to a far-off acquaintance, but these small pieces are the fibers that make up the strong support network.

Nevertheless, the method of finding allies does not always face various hurdles. Critics and naysayers can come out, and they contest the vision and determination of the entrepreneur. The point is that criticism should be seen not as a discour-agement but as a way to develop. Negative feedback can be converted to a positive contribution by the use of mental models and reframing techniques. It is this toughness that ends up enhancing the entrepreneurial spirit itself and makes it possible to sail through the turbulence in the process of estab-lishing a business with cemented assurance and grace.

The entrepreneurial journey is one of continuous learning and adaptation. By seeking out allies in unexpected places, entre-preneurs not only expand their network but also enrich their perspective. These connections serve as a testament to the power of community and collaboration, highlighting that suc-cess is not a solitary endeavor but a collective achievement. As these alliances form and evolve, they become the cornerstone of a resilient and dynamic entrepreneurial ecosystem, one that thrives on diversity and innovation.

Handling Naysayers

Hate and doubt are unavoidable friends in the entrepreneurial journey, and knowing this can change how you deal with de-tractors. You are about to take the plunge into a new business, excited and maybe even trepidation, when suddenly you are assaulted by the doubts of those who surround you. This situation is no exception, and it is essential to understand that it is a natural part of the entrepreneurial process.

An example of a story that a reader told depicts this perfectly: when starting their own business, both their family and their colleagues were doubtful. It can be a lonely experience, but it is an entrepreneurial rite of passage. The trick will be to reframe such criticism constructively.

First of all, a practical mental model can be used, the so-called feedback filter. This practice entails the recognition of useful feedback among the noise so that entrepreneurs can concen-trate on fruitful feedback without being dragged into the pit of pessimism. The need to sort criticism into types and match them with the most appropriate response strategies will enable entrepreneurs to remain calm and professional. As an exam-ple, a dismissive comment posted on LinkedIn can be re-sponded to with a non-emotional response or an email tem-plate of thank you for your comments.

Another necessary step is to process the emotional fallout of criticism. The prompts of reflection used in rituals of gaining confidence and moving on may be: What is the kernel of truth, if any, in this feedback? By presenting these criticisms to a group of peers, one may get a new outlook on the matter and transform what earlier appeared rude into a chance of becoming better.

Moreover, by reinterpreting negative reviews or feedback as a chance to improve a product feature, it is possible to change the attitude of defeat to one of improvement. This not only creates resilience but also creates a spirit of entrepreneurship that survives on continuous improvement and learning.

When dealing with the naysayers, one must be optimistic and realistic at the same time. This compromise means that, as long as hope is not lost, the decisions made are also evidence-based. By using such instruments as the Optimism-Realism Matrix, the score of optimism versus realism can be deter-mined in relation to the key decisions, which is a good tool to evaluate the risks and not to lose sight of the goals.

Finally, one should develop resilience toward naysayers by developing a strong support system. Such practices as sharing wins and losses with a small circle of people can be priceless. Such groups are not only accountable but also offer individu-als a platform to process feedback constructively.

Creating a mental attitude, Mastery of my own, is creating the ability to maintain growth and intent regardless of criticism. With these practices integrated into day-to-day activities, busi-ness people can use the possible failures as stepping stones to success. Please keep in mind that the entrepreneurial journey is as much a journey of resilience and flexibility as it is of innova-tion and creativity. Instead of flowing with criticism as a hin-drance, it can be used as a way to grow, thus turning critics into unintentionally helpful people in your pursuit of success.

Building Community Online

Entrepreneurship is moving toward the intersection of the physical and the virtual realm in the digital age, and the oppor-tunities of creating meaningful communities are enormous. The online community terrain presents a mosaic of possibili-ties to entrepreneurs in need of broadening their networks, acquiring insights, and building partnerships. Websites like Slack, Indie Hackers, and LinkedIn have become critical spaces in which entrepreneurs can not just navigate but also prosper as a result of the experience and resources shared.

The initial aspect of taking advantage of such platforms is the knowledge of the culture and focus of each. Slack, which is characterized by its real-time communication and collaborative features, enables the entrepreneur to participate in the channels related to the specific niche where the conversation could be intensive and broad. Instead, Indie Hackers is more of a fo-rum-style platform that offers entrepreneurs a chance to talk about their experience, their struggles, and their successes, and helps foster a culture of openness and helpfulness. With its professional connection background, LinkedIn provides a more formal solution to community development in which acquaintances may result in mentoring, partnerships, and busi-ness.

In order to realize the potential of these online communities, the entrepreneurs should not act on them as observers but as participants. This entails being authentic when presenting one-self, giving contributions, and engaging in discussions in a manner that adds value to the community. A good plan in-volves writing a convincing intro post that brings out one's experience, struggles, and points where guidance is required. This not only makes the entrepreneur an active member of the community but also makes significant friendships and part-nerships.

The participation in these communities ought to be tactical and regular. Entrepreneurs are able to create the utmost value by engaging in events such as Ask Me Anything (AMA) sessions, feedback threads, and virtual meetups. Through these interac-tions, there is visibility where entrepreneurs can demonstrate their knowledge and collect varied views about their business-es. Rituals like sharing weekly wins, finding accountability part-ners, and volunteering to help other people help cement one-self and credibility in the community even more.

In addition to personal relationships, entrepreneurs can take advantage of the systematic application of digital tools to structure and coordinate their relationships in the community. An electronic networking locator, e.g., can also be useful to keep track of the contacts, interactions, and follow-ups. This orderly approach gives a sense that not only are engagements important but also produce tangible results, including partner-ships, collaborations, or mentorships.

There are no challenges to building an online community. Entrepreneurs have to walk the fine line of adding value with-out the traps of over-selling or passive loitering. It all depends on developing authentic relationships, where relationships are developed but not transactional relationships. When entrepre-neurs start being immersed in these digital ecosystems, they develop a support network that is certainly as valuable as any traditional business network.

After all, the process of developing a community online is about establishing the environment in which business people will learn, share, and prosper. It is concerning the use of intel-ligence and vitality of like-minded people who share common objectives and dreams. Through active participation in these communities, entrepreneurs are both empowering themselves and advancing a greater wave of innovation and collaboration amid the digital era.

CREATIVE PROBLEM SOLVING

The Constraint Advantage

The existence of limitations is usually viewed as a drag on in-genuity and a hindrance to possibilities in the environment of entrepreneurship. However, from a new perspective, the same limitations can be effective sources of creative power and in-genuity. The idea of jugaad or innovation, common in re-source-scarcity settings, is an example of how constraints can be turned into a strategic opportunity. This strategy motivates entrepreneurs to be creative in using what they have and not regretting what they do not have.

The capability to reframe obstacles as opportunities is one of the fundamental values of leveraging constraints. This change of mindset is essential to entrepreneurs who, in most instanc-es, have limited resources, be it financial, technological, or hu-man resources. The lack of resources makes it necessary to concentrate on the key aspects, depriving the non-vital and emphasizing the essence of the value offered by a venture. This emphasis does not just simplify activities, but also pre-pares a culture of thriftiness and effectiveness.

A good example is that of a bootstrapped software-as-a-service (SaaS) startup that was able to make it with little fund-ing. With the minimalism concept, the founder could focus on coming up with a product that was purely responsive to cus-tomer needs, without any distractions caused by unnecessary features. This emphasis on core functionality saw to it that every development decision would be related to the produc-tion of the greatest value to the users, culminating in a profita-ble and sustainable business model.

In addition, there is the concept of Asset Mapping, which can help reveal the hidden or unused assets that can prove decisive in battling limitations. The method here is to list the available skills, relationships, and tools so as to determine what poten-tial assets can be used to develop the business. As an example, it may be possible to convert a personal network into a set of beta testers and, in such a way, get the feedback and confirma-tion that is invaluable and does not require much spending on the part of the entrepreneur.

The other outcome of constraint-based thinking is the embra-sure of innovative methods of solving problems. Being lim-ited, entrepreneurs are forced to find new solutions that would not have been thought of in an abundance of resources. It is this need-based innovation that tends to give rise to break-through ideas that transform industry standards and develop competitive advantages.

Also, constraints promote exploration and trial-and-error. Entrepreneurs have fewer resources and thus will tend to conduct micro-experiments to prove or disprove assumptions and obtain feedback within a short time. This cyclic procedure not only enhances the speed of learning and adaptation but also reduces risk because small-scale testing can be performed, and it does not require a lot of investment. Having a lean ap-proach allows entrepreneurs to pivot quickly based on market feedback, where the solutions can be relevant and effective.

Fundamentally, the constraint advantage is that it contributes to resilience and flexibility. Entrepreneurs who learn the disci-pline of constraint-based innovation can be in a better place to cope with the intricacies of a constantly evolving business environment. They are taught to see limitations not as an end, but as a way to be creative and strive. This culture not only improves their problem-solving skills but also creates a culture of ongoing improvement and nimbleness.

Finally, the benefit of constraint is approximately turning con-straints into successful tools. Through embracing constraints, businesspeople can open up a treasure trove of creative power, making a challenge a stepping stone to long-term growth and success.

Pain Point Interviews

To lead to any meaningful innovation, it is essential to know the fundamental problems that the potential customers experi-ence to avoid the trap of developing a solution to a problem that does not exist. The process of pain point interviews is an essential mechanism to dig up these authentic challenges, and this way, any entrepreneurial undertaking is informed by the real-life needs and not imaginary ones.

A problem-first approach is promoted as an alternative to leaping to solutions. This is a technique that entails digging deep into the lives and disappointments of your target audi-ence via well-organized interviews. These discussions ought to be structured in such a way that they are free and free-flowing without imposing any form of leading questions that may distort the responses. A well-crafted interview script may have some open-ended questions that are broad in nature and en-courage the interviewee to expound on the details of his or her experience, as the interviewer does not restrict him/her to a fixed set of questions.

Scheduling of these interviews can be achieved by using a straightforward outreach message that makes it clear that you need it and that their input is valuable. When such discussions are afoot, it is not only to listen but also to listen actively and see what themes and patterns in the described issues stand out. It is in this pattern recognition that the best opportunities to be found in innovation lie. The ranking and combination of these pain points in one group will allow entrepreneurs to focus on the most urgent and, consequently, the most profita-ble ones to work with.

In order to be in control of the insights that one obtains through these interviews, a powerful system that can capture, organize, and share this information is necessary. One can use tools such as Notion or Google Sheets to keep an organized database of interview notes, which can be easily accessed and updated as new information is discovered. This type of system can be useful in the present project as well as a useful source in the future, as information storage or as a source for a partner or co-founder.

In addition, the conclusions made on the basis of these inter-views are directly translated into the idea validation process. It is by knowing what exact issues the users have that the entre-preneurs can create specific solutions and then, within minutes, test their feasibility with no-code tools. This devel-opment and feedback process is repeated to make sure the solutions are not only created to meet the real needs, but they are also created in a way that appeals to the target audience.

Pain point interviews, in a word, form one of the fundamental parts of the entrepreneurial toolkit. They give the unfiltered feedback that is required to push innovation towards a path that is meaningful and sustainable. Through the discovery of genuine problems using these interviews, entrepreneurs are placed in a position of developing products and services that are not only demanded but that are enthusiastically adopted by the people they target.

Idea Validation in 24 Hours

Noting the rapid nature of the environment in the field of entrepreneurship, the skill to rapidly test ideas takes prece-dence. It saves time and resources and offers a strong base on which to proceed in the future with confidence. It is a potent resource to entrepreneurs, and the validation of an idea in 24 hours enables people to test their assumptions and receive feedback based on actual conditions without necessarily hav-ing to code or develop much.

The essence of this approach is the use of no-code tools, which make it possible to democratize digital products. Carrd, Bubble, and Airtable provide easy-to-use tools to create work-ing prototypes. The tools allow entrepreneurs to build landing pages or barebones applications that can form the front end of their product ideas. The ease and expediency of these plat-forms are essential since they can be used without any tech-nical obstacles.

The 24-hour validation challenge is an organized task that enables entrepreneurs to go through the early phases of evalu-ating an entrepreneurship idea. Creation of a landing page within the first two hours is the starting point. The page is a virtual shop window, a preview of the product/service to a prospective customer. The trick is to prepare meaningful mes-saging that brings the value proposition out clearly. Calls to action and sample copy are required to guide user interest and engagement.

The second stage after developing the landing page is to traffic the page. This may be done using many avenues, including social media advertisements, email, or other networks. This is aimed at reaching a wide audience on the landing page, and the period of time during this stage is between three and six hours. Traffic collection is one of the important activities be-cause it preconditions the most important step of validation, which is user feedback.

When the day continues, between the time of seven hours and twenty-four hours, the emphasis is on examining the interac-tions and reactions of the users. This step is concerned with gauging engagement in the form of sign-ups, inquiries, and feedback forms. Such data points give practical information on market interest and whether the idea can be viable. Entre-preneurs are advised to perform smoke tests, e.g., fake door testing, in which they test interest by posting a call-to-action, which results in an explanation that the product is still in de-velopment.

The information obtained at this time is priceless. It provides a candid evaluation of the attractiveness of the idea and points out its weak points. This feedback is then to be interpreted by the entrepreneurs in order to recycle and improve their ideas. This cycle has the advantage of refining the idea according to real-world feedback, which gives it a much better chance to succeed.

The expedited character of this type of validation not only short-circuits the decision-making process but also fosters the spirit of agility and responsiveness. Entrepreneurial culture: entrepreneurs get to learn to act based on facts, but not as-sumptions, and they take on the culture of continuous im-provement and innovation. At the expiry of the 24 hours, the entrepreneur would have a better idea of the market fit of their idea and make informed decisions regarding their venture on whether to pursue, pivot, or pause.

Finally, the 24-hour concept of the validation system is an ode to the strength of contemporary business instruments and practices. It highlights the value of speed and flexibility in the current fast-paced business world. It prepares the entrepreneur with the ability to manoeuvre through the uncertainty with confidence and clarity.

Real-Time Resilience

With the hectic nature of entrepreneurship, it is essential to have the flexibility to adjust and recover after failure. This is commonly known as real-time resilience and is concerned with developing an attitude in which challenges are viewed not as an insurmountable obstacle but as an opportunity to grow. Real-time resilience is the act of controlling the reaction to failure as a stepping stone to success in the future.

One of the tools that can be used to establish real-time resili-ence is the so-called Fail Log, which is a dynamic document to which entrepreneurs are advised to keep. The log is an account of the day-to-day or weekly failures, what has gone wrong, and, what is more significant, what has been learned during the experience. When the failures are sorted by type and se-verity, including such categories as "Execution Error," "Market Misread," or "External Forces," the entrepreneur can discover the patterns and common problems that require solution.

Maintaining a Fail Log is not merely a matter of listing the failures; it is a matter of celebrating productive failures. This would imply acknowledging the milestones that have been achieved through trial and error, as opposed to concentrating only on the bad side of failure. Entrepreneurs are invited to consider such "Failure Wins" each month and identify what they learn about themselves or their log entries. This reflection practice converts the failures into a motivation and learning resource that leads to steady advancement and innovation.

It is also possible to increase learning and resilience by sharing Fail Logs with accountability partners or even in mastermind groups. Discussing the setbacks within an encouraging society will enable entrepreneurs to acquire different views and con-structive criticism. This shared consideration not only enables a better processing of failures but also creates an open, open-to-growth culture.

Besides the Fail Log, energizing and concentration rituals play a critical role in overcoming the issue of entrepreneurial burn-out, which is a widespread problem in the sphere. It is of par-amount importance to identify the symptoms of burnout at the earliest possible stage; among them, one can distinguish such issues as chronic fatigue, irritability, and reduced produc-tivity. In order to overcome these impacts, the entrepreneurs are mentored to embrace evidence-based rituals in their prac-tices. Some of the techniques recommended include the 90-Minute Reset, which means having deep rest and creativity recharging periods at designated intervals. Conscious change practices, such as short breathwork or movement exercises, aid in keeping the mind clear and the mood stable.

Digital detox practices are also encouraged, so the entrepre-neur should establish limits and set their own time off, even when they are in high-pressure periods. As an example, mak-ing a vow of No-Work Sundays or email-free evenings can have a potent effect at helping improve mental health and avoiding burnout. With such precautionary measures, the business people will be able to stay energized and focus on their long-term objectives.

In real-time resilience practice, entrepreneurs are not only taught to be in the continuous ups and downs of the journey but also to establish a strong foundation to continue their success and self-improvement. They develop an attitude that is tough, flexible, and innovation-ready by perceiving failures as part of the learning process.

CHAPTER 6

DECISION-MAKING DURING UNCER-TAINTY

The Uncertainty Toolkit

The realm of entrepreneurship is an inseparable companion of uncertainty. To navigate through the fog of the unknowns, he or she should possess not only courage but also a tool set that contains the strategies that may help him or her predict and adapt to the various circumstances. Entrepreneurs often find themselves in crossroads scenarios in which everyone is re-quired to make decisions without having all the information. It is here that scenario mapping can be a very useful process. By visualizing the possible futures, the entrepreneur will be ready for the best and worst scenarios and offer a roadmap that would help him/her navigate the possible obstacles.

The start of scenario mapping begins with a clear picture of your business environment. It would be recommended that the entrepreneurs sketch a basic scenario map that would be subdivided into different outcomes based on specific choices and events. Using such a visualization, one can observe the chain effects of their choices and can learn more about poten-tial advantages and pitfalls. As an indicator, the map can be suggested to increase the intensity of marketing activity when the first group of customers rates a product as satisfactory. Quite to the contrary, if the feedback is not that enthusiastic, the map may translate into the need to enhance the product features.

This toolkit cannot be carried out without the identification of the critical assumptions and triggers that can destroy them. Entrepreneurs ought to ask themselves questions, some of them being, what is the assumption that the business model is being built on, and what would signify that I need to change. This is a proactive move where they are not caught unaware of changes in market behavior or consumer behavior. To moni-tor such variability as it arises, an Assumptions vs. Triggers table comes in handy, providing a methodical response to the variability.

A toolkit also exists to create a scenario map that would be tailored to a specific business setting. The entrepreneur utilizes the templates as a starting point in establishing their own tracks in view of their unique difficulties and prospects. One of the final scenario maps, one of the ones that is applied to the introduction of a new SaaS feature, can be inspirational and educational.

Besides, there is a Pivot or Persevere checklist that is offered to business owners. Such a framework of the decision-making process will assist in observing whether to continue on track or make a strategic change. Based on these clear kill criteria and pivot triggers, deciding to venture into new projects ahead of time will assist entrepreneurs in making informed decisions without being influenced by the emotional attachment they have to the projects they are venturing into. These checklist items might include: Have you met a learning milestone? Or, is it a key metric on an upward trend, or is it not?

The concepts are put into real life with practical examples on how entrepreneurs have used these tools successfully in mak-ing complex decisions. An individual founder can switch di-rections following a trail of adverse remarks, but a group can continue and thrive following slight readjustments on the same path.

Entrepreneurs ought to create a troubleshooting guide in or-der to avoid the common traps in decision-making, such as the sunk cost trap or over-optimism. This is a manual for the potential traps, and gives the means by which they can be avoided, and a culture of informed and flexible decision-making can be established.

The Uncertainty Toolkit is not simply risk management; in general, it is empowering entrepreneurs to make their own choices. With the uncertainty being accepted as the part and parcel of the entrepreneurial course, they can transform the probable problems into drivers of progress and innovation.

The Pivot or Persevere Checklist

Due to the dynamic character of entrepreneurship, decisions tend to be premised on the fulcrum of pivot or persevere. It is a very important juncture at which the entrepreneur must make the decision either to deviate or continue the path already fol-lowed by the enterprise. This is not an intuitive process, but it is a process that is somewhat founded on systematic evalua-tion and reflection. The use of a checklist-based decision-making model will serve as a guide during such a time of con-fusion and will provide entrepreneurs with the path they are to use to go through the business development storm.

The purpose of this framework is to identify the existence of a learning milestone. This involves intense consideration of key metrics in order to indicate either improvement or stagnation. Those are not only figures but the stamp of progress, perfor-mance, and acceptance in the market. The key can guarantee the success or stagnation of understanding and interpretation of such signals.

There should be clear triggers and kill criteria, which are to be put in place before the new initiatives are initiated. These pre-concerted standards are the safeguards of emotional decision-making in that they are founded on empirical evidence rather than hope and fear. An example is that a startup might decide that within the first month, it will have to rebrand its value in case it fails to attract 100 users. This kind of strategic foresight prevents wastage of resources and time since the business can respond to the market needs promptly.

The mini-case studies will give a clue to the practice of the checklist. Take a glimpse at the story of a solitary creator who had consistently gotten unfavorable feedback and chose to pivot. This decision was made on the basis of the good-faith consideration of user feedback, which, ultimately, led to the more successful business model. Conversely, the other team was patient because they had not made any significant chang-es, but had rather made little adjustments, and with time, they ended up achieving the intended growth. These narrations focus on the necessity of being adaptable and receptive to matters of entrepreneurship.

Other decision-making traps that an entrepreneur must be wary of include the sunk cost fallacy, over-optimism, and fear of change. The troubleshooting guide is a manual that helps individuals avoid these psychological traps. Being conscious of the signs of these pitfalls, the entrepreneurs will be able to avoid them and make sensible and reasonable choices to achieve success in the long run within the business.

The Traps and How to Break Free table provides measures that should be followed to overcome these psychological ob-stacles. To illustrate the point, considering the sunk costs of the creation of a product can help allow a team to venture into new, potentially more productive directions as well.

Lastly, the pivot or persevere checklist is one such tool that is also an attitude. It cultivates the spirit of lifelong learning and change that makes entrepreneurs agile in regard to change. This framework can enable businesses to respond to risks and opportunities as they arise in a better position because they have adopted this in their strategic planning. This also results in resilience and provides the entrepreneurs with confidence in their decisions since they are assured of a powerful system to fall back on when they are in an uncertain state.

Risk Radar

The way to predict and handle risks is one of the most im-portant skills that an entrepreneur should develop in the com-plex world of entrepreneurship. This is a skill commonly known as risk radar, and it is the ability to build a sense of identifying a possible trap and knowing what it means, both on the personal and business level. It is making a plan to an-ticipate and mitigate the issues that may bring down the mo-mentum or damage the business.

Entrepreneurs are frequently heroised on the basis of their daring and readiness to take risks. Still, it is the entrepreneurs who combine audacity with a systematic approach to risk who are most successful. Identification of the potential risks and their classification are the first steps towards creating a Risk Radar. This would entail the examination of different aspects of the business, including financial weaknesses, reputational risks, technical risks, team dynamics, and legal risks. Each cat-egory must be mapped onto a radar chart and visualize where the most vulnerabilities occur, with the possibility of focusing strategically on the areas that need urgent attention.

The next step is to quantify and prioritize the existence of these risks, and this includes understanding the probability and the effect of any potential problem. One of the tools that would be useful in this process is a risk matrix, which would allow the entrepreneur to rate risks on the basis of their likeli-hood and possible harm. Such a scoring system is useful in separating high-priority risks that require urgent attention and low-priority risks that can be observed over time.

After identifying and ranking the risks, it is necessary to come up with contingency plans. These are the so-called Plan B plans designed to respond to all high-priority risks in case they happen. As an example, should one of the major issues be the shortage of cash, the backup strategy could involve acquiring a line of credit or finding cost-reduction options that can be enforced within a short period of time. On the same note, where there are chances that negative publicity is involved, the presence of a crisis communication plan can help avert the harm to the reputation of the company.

Monitoring and updating the Risk Radar should be regular since the world of business is dynamic and in a process of constant change. Regular check-ins and updates on the risk management strategies used by entrepreneurs should be in-corporated so that these strategies stay pertinent and effective. The continuous operation of this process assists in remaining proactive but not reactive and making quick changes as new threats or existing threats are formed or developed.

To make it possible, it is possible to organize a monthly "Risk Review" during which the risk scores will be reconsidered, and the efficacy of the existing mitigation strategies will be evaluat-ed. The alliance of the core team members in this review is essential since the different opinions and knowledge would be advantageous in this regard. Also, it is important to keep a checklist on revisiting and updating the risk scores to ensure that the Risk Radar is a living document that develops along with the business.

Overall, the creation of a strong Risk Radar is the process of building a culture of alertness and readiness in the company. It entails training oneself and the team to be critical in thinking about the possible risks and to handle them systematically. Through this, the entrepreneurs will be more confident in going about business knowing that they are in a position to deal with challenges before they escalate to crises. Not only does this foresight and preparation help to secure the busi-ness, it also gives the entrepreneur the confidence to take risks more confidently, knowing that he has a well-laid-out strategy on how to handle the risks that are bound to come along with innovation and expansion.

Balancing Data and Instinct

When it comes to entrepreneurship, the choices made may consistently be based on the oscillation between the extremes of data analysis and the nudges induced by intuition. Entre-preneurs often have to be at this crossroads, where cold rea-soning of figures collides with warm intuition of experience. The conflict between the two powers is not merely an issue but a distinctive feature of effective entrepreneurial decision-making.

The facts and figures used in data speak with the authority of data and provide a pretence of certainty in a world that is un-predictable in nature. It offers the measures according to which success is frequently determined and enables entrepre-neurs to monitor the achievements, determine the tendencies, and evaluate the results. Data is appealing because of its objec-tivity; it is an instrument that can be utilized to legitimize deci-sions, obtain investments, and optimize strategies. However, data itself can be a two-sided sword, as it can result in analysis paralysis, and information overload can be employed as a hindrance to action.

Conversely, intuition, which is often considered a simple gut feeling, is essential in manoeuvring the ambiguity and speed at which the entrepreneurial ventures would change. Intuition is the summary of experience, the synthesis of knowledge that we make unconsciously, and which determines choices in cas-es when there is not enough, or none, of the necessary infor-mation. It is the inner barometer of the entrepreneur, which has been developed through years of experience, failures, and achievements.

Penetration is no game of zero sum when it comes to the interaction between data and instinct. Enlightened entrepre-neurs know how to strike a balance between these forces and know when to tilt on one side rather than the other. This bal-ance tends to give rise to practical heuristics, or rules of thumb. An example of these would be a rule indicating that you should do something based on the consistent feedback of several customers, or that you should take quick action when a decision can be easily reversed. Such heuristics give a guideline on how to make fast and competent decisions without finding oneself bogged down by data analysis details.

Realistically, this balance is reached by a process of reflection and readjustment. Entrepreneurs may utilize both data analysis and gut-check exercises, and compare what the numbers are telling them with what their gut is telling them. Such a twofold methodology enables a more subtle decision-making proce-dure, one that is directed by empirical evidence, as well as per-sonal interpretation.

The history of entrepreneurship is full of tales of people who managed to find the right balance. Please think of the founder who disregarded the piles of user feedback to follow his or her hunch and emerged victorious, or of the founder who acted on the basis of data alone and ignored his or her gut. These anecdotes lead to recognition of the need to not only have access to the data, but also know when to trust his or her gut.

Finally, the art of data-instinct balance is about developing a mentality that appreciates both. It demands readiness both to learn by numbers and by experience, and to revise or refine personal heuristics as time passes. As entrepreneurial activities become larger and their businesses more complex, so does their capacity to combine data with intuition, forming a deci-sion-making process that is not only rigorous but also adap-tive and grounded, but imaginative. This is not merely a skill but a state of mind, and it can turn uncertainty into opportuni-ty, intuition into insight.

CHAPTER 7

SUSTAINING GROWTH AND PURPOSE

The Optimism-Realism Balance

In business entrepreneurship, balancing between pessimism and realism is essential in maintaining a winning business. This balance is not just a philosophical point but a practical model that correlates with decision-making, risk evaluation, and stra-tegic planning.

Without hope, there would be no entrepreneurial spirit, and so that would give a person enough strength to take up projects that would be considered too risky by others. It is this attitude that motivates entrepreneurs to think big, innovate, and chal-lenge limits. Optimism also helps build resilience, which makes an entrepreneur persevere in the face of frustration and diffi-culties. It is the fuel that brings the vision back to life and makes entrepreneurs look beyond short-term challenges and look at long-term goals.

However, unbridled optimism can cause overconfidence, poor decision-making, and misguided strategic moves. It is at this point that realism is of importance. Realism is a stabilizing factor, whereby optimism does not cause entrepreneurship to turn blindly to the possibility of risks and difficulties. It in-cludes an objective evaluation of the prevailing state of affairs and market dynamics, as well as checks on the viability of business plans.

The interaction between optimism and realism can be imag-ined by using the approach of the Optimism-Realism Matrix. This tool is aimed at helping entrepreneurs rate their decisions according to these two parameters. This matrix will help moti-vate the entrepreneurs to review their plans by looking at the bright as well as the realistic side of their decisions. In this way, they will be able to find out where they tend to be overly op-timistic and where a more realistic approach is justified.

To illustrate, in the case of a product launch, an entrepreneur may be hopeful of the reception in the market. Nevertheless, an objective evaluation would include an analysis of the market data, getting insight into customer needs, and reflecting on possible challenges. The two prongs assist in designing strate-gies that are not merely visionary in essence but workable at the same time.

As part of this balance, entrepreneurs are advised to engage in routine optimism audits, which are reflective practices in which entrepreneurs are advised to recognize biases that can influ-ence their decision-making. This is done by asking yourself the question: What is the risk that I am not paying enough atten-tion to at this moment? Or have I not thought of everything? These audits can also serve to recalibrate strategies so that they are consistent with both ambitions and reality.

Further, it is possible to create a Balanced Decision Ritual that will help business people make wise decisions. This entails enumerating hopes, fears, available information, and subse-quent actions prior to making decisions. Businessmen and women can make optimistic and realistic decisions by system-atically reviewing the best, worst, and most probable scenarios.

Finally, there is a need to balance between optimism and real-ism in order to run a sustainable entrepreneurship. It lets the entrepreneur have big dreams without losing sight of reality, thus making them navigate the business world complexities with ease and certainty. Combining the two views, entrepre-neurs will be able to establish strong businesses that can with-stand change and embrace opportunities when they come along.

Ethical Decision-Making

During such a complicated game of entrepreneurship, ethical decision-making is one of the keys to sustainable prosperity. Sometimes entrepreneurs have to make their way through morally uncertain circumstances, especially when their busi-nesses expand and include the lives of more people. Such dilemmas may extend to addressing the privacy of the users, layoff issues, and deceptive marketing. The complexities of these situations require a strong model that will direct decision-making procedures in a manner that is ethical and transparent.

A practical approach to the ethical decision-making process is based on the use of a systematic framework that considers various aspects of a decision. The Four-Filter ethical checklist is one of the useful ones. This checklist promotes decisions that the entrepreneurs make in terms of legality, transparency, impact on stakeholders, and long-term impacts. These filters make it possible to recognize the ethical soundness of deci-sions made by entrepreneurs. The systematic application of the latter guarantees the consistency of their actions both with the law and with moral values.

The real-life experiences of ethical decision-making normally show the subtle difficulties that entrepreneurs encounter. As an example, in the case of a potentially profitable partnership potentially involving the breach of user information, the checklist will trigger the re-evaluation of possible legal conse-quences and clarity of the agreement. Moreover, it presuppos-es the evaluation of the possible effect of stakeholders such as customers, workforce, and investors, and considers the repu-tation of the company in the long run.

On top of structures, there is the development of a culture of ethics in the entrepreneurial ecosystem. This entails the in-built rituals and scripts that strengthen value-based decision-making even when pressure is mounted. An example is to perform an ethics check-in prior to the launch of products or a meeting with investors, which can be an important moment of reflec-tion to ensure that product decisions are not purely about profits, but rather rooted in ethics.

Ethical standards are valuable not only in evading the traps of the law. Organisations that encourage ethical decision-making tend to receive both increased customer trust and employee loyalty. An example is a startup that opts to be transparent, which can end in a robust customer base that appreciates honesty and integrity, and as a result, long-term success. On the other hand, ethically insensitive ventures can receive a neg-ative response as it can be countered by the general society, which negatively impacts their image and destroys their stake-holders.

Mini-case studies on businesses that have successfully or failed to overcome ethical dilemmas can also be used to train entre-preneurs. A single narrative may feature a start-up that success-fully gained large-scale customer trust by acting with transpar-ency. In contrast, the other one may be a description of a ven-ture that had issues with its ethical conduct and consequently experienced reputational losses. Such stories are not only cau-tionary but also are great reminders of the value of ethics in the business world.

Finally, ethical decision-making is not an isolated event, but a process of staying true to yourself. It demands that business-people should be more alert to re-examine their strategies and choices in an ethical sense. With such an atmosphere of ensur-ing that ethical considerations take priority, entrepreneurs will find it far easier to deal with the gray areas of business with confidence and integrity, and even have their businesses play a positive role in society, while ensuring that they grow sustaina-bly.

Tracking Your Mindset Shifts

Adaptation and personal development are the most important aspects of the constantly changing world of entrepreneurship. This is an important component in maintaining personal and professional development, as you are able to follow your atti-tudes as time progresses. It is an attentive, thoughtful exercise of noticing and recording changes in your mental state and using contemporary digital technology to facilitate the process.

Think of being able to trace the development of your mindset, as though you are making graphs of your advancement in any of your fields of life. This is a visualization that can be accom-plished through the use of digital tools like Notion, Google Sheets, or advanced journaling apps. On these sites, you can create visual dashboards that summarize your experience with measurements of your mood, the actions you took, and your confidence. Not only do such dashboards make progress concrete, but they are also a great motivator for how much progress one has made.

The establishment of such digital notifications and checks of progress can greatly support new habits. Weekly or monthly self-review reminders will be automatically sent to remind you of your progress and where you have fallen short. This check-in assists in cementing new habitual approaches to the mind-set and makes these changes not only permanent but also ingrained into your entrepreneurial persona.

In addition, celebrating milestones is a part of this tracking process. The creation of a system to celebrate mindset achievements will stimulate the review of progress and will give a feeling of achievement. It may include stopping in with a mentor or an accountability group, where, besides legitimizing your progress, it also provides access to supportive feedback and encouragement.

The process of mindset change tracking is not an easy task, involving recording the changes but also getting to know what underlies those changes. It is the process of defining the expe-riences, struggles, and wins that make you develop a changing mindset. In so doing, you are able to build a story, which will not just map your progress, but also equip you with a strong and flexible attitude towards life in the future.

Practically, this method consists of establishing a workflow in which you frequently check your progress. You could also evaluate your changes in mindset at the end of each quarter, with the help of asking yourself some critical questions: What have I learned? What are the new insights that I have acquired? What were the obstacles I was able to overcome, and how did they change my mindset?

It is also a practice of reflection and is further supported by the practice of rituals that glorify your progress. These rituals may involve a quarterly review of mindset milestones and a celebration where you celebrate your success and set new tar-gets. This consolidates good changes and encourages further development and adjustment.

Finally, the process of tracking mindset changes is concerned with the development of awareness of your personal devel-opment process. It makes you active in making progress and allows you to enjoy tracking your development with the help of digital tools. It is a process that helps to develop an attitude of constant development, the ability to withstand and face the dynamic environment of business, and readiness to respond to the changes within it.

Designing Your Life

Consider that your life is a painting, and each line is a con-scious decision; each color is some other element of your life. This canvas is turned into a colorful tapestry by the entrepre-neurial mind, where personal ambitions blend with the work-ing ones. When you get up every morning, you have a growth question as your muse, which directs your mind and actions to the path of continual improvement. It is a basic ritual that can make you look inward and ask yourself how you can broaden your horizons today, both by knowing something new or changing your worldview.

During the less dramatic moments of the night, contemplation is a strong weapon. This is where you narrate the dangers you have encountered and the lessons learnt, and you use them as one stepping stone on your road. It is not a mere routine but a pledge to self-development, a pledge to yourself to always be receptive to the multitude of options of life through this daily practice of reflection.

Business is not the only sphere where the entrepreneurial mentality can be applied; it is a flexible model that can improve all aspects of life. It may be personal goals or professional goals, but a balance between these goals is achieved through alignment. A weekly planning template will become your guide, in which personal and professional development is combined with the objectives and key results (OKRs). The provided structured approach guarantees that there is nothing in your life that is left unattended, and this would create a holistic growth environment.

Another aspect of such a mindset is life experiments, which urge you to leave the limits of the routine. Every month pro-vides a fresh chance to do something new, whether it be a skill, hobby, or routine, and make the banal seem like a play-ground. These experiments are not simply the process of gaining new skills but about the pain of the unknown and learning to enjoy the learning process.

The entrepreneurial mind also spills over to the outside and affects the way we treat communities and family. When we use the concepts of entrepreneurship in these fields, we end up creating an environment that flourishes in innovation and sustainability. This attitude helps us view difficulties as a source of learning to help usher in an environment where creativity and problem-solving blossom.

The entrepreneurial thinking in design will become your guid-ing light in the process of living your life. It gives you the will to be in charge, be the one who comes up with his or her own fate. The ritual of posing the growth question in the morning turns into a daily reminder about your willingness to develop personally. In contrast, the evening reflection will be a testi-monial to your strength and flexibility.

With these practices incorporated into your day-to-day lives, you end up living a life not just successful but also an enrich-ing one. Every day is another chapter in your own life story, the story of struggle and victory. In this sense, life is not a sequence of solitary events but a united process leading to self-actualization.

Finally, the entrepreneurial attitude challenges you to lead a purposeful life and act in a way that supports your values and ideals. It is a request to shape your life into a masterpiece, one brushstroke, a decision in the great painting of your life. It is because of this attitude that you create a life filled with meaning and potential, the power of intentional living.

FROM BURNOUT TO BREAKTHROUGH

The Grit Audit

In entrepreneurship, it is the skill to be able to quickly move back on your feet after a downfall and soldier on. It is a con-troversial notion commonly known as grit, which is a decisive factor in the success of an entrepreneur. The Grit Audit is a reflective instrument that is aimed at assisting entrepreneurs in evaluating their flexibility and ability to evolve to face challeng-es. This self-assessment is not just like the common personali-ty tests; rather, it dwells on the real-life issues of tenacity and reaction to misfortune.

The Grit Audit is a sequence of twelve specific questions that explore the capacity to endure hardships, flexibility in the face of changing realities, and the quality of the reaction to failure. These questions are designed to show personal grit deficien-cies, spots where an entrepreneur may require more strength or nimbleness. It is based on these gaps that entrepreneurs can shape their strategies against these weaknesses to advance their resilience to failures or setbacks.

To enable this self-evaluation, the Grit Audit proposes a scor-ing scale that distinctly characterizes persons as either a Steady Sprinter, a person capable of sustaining momentum short-term, a Resilient Grinder, a person who persists through thick and thin, or a Momentum Seeker, someone who lives by the motto of never standing still. These archetypes assist entre-preneurs in determining their inherent behaviors and how they can maximise their strengths whilst taking into consideration their weaknesses.

This audit involves the use of reflection. Entrepreneurs are challenged to explore previous experiences by remembering the times when they have recovered fast and at other times when they have not. This self-reflexivity is essential to identify-ing the patterns in behavior and reaction, which offers an understanding of how they could tackle subsequent issues more efficiently.

The Grit Audit also provides possible micro-habits that entre-preneurs may implement to become grittier. The habits can be small but doable activities like choosing to dedicate time every day to a five-minute frustration reset to help them quickly get over minor frustrations, or creating a Setback Story Bank where they can write down and reflect on the lessons learned from their past failures. These practices do not just enhance resilience but also instill an attitude that is oriented towards learning and development.

In addition, the Grit Audit suggests a way of monitoring the grit development in the long term. With the help of such tools as the Grit Growth Chart, entrepreneurs will be able to see their progress, and they will observe the way their capacity to recover after a setback is improving and how fast they can get back on their feet after failing. This constant monitoring can be used as a motivator, and it can be used to keep an entre-preneur developing their ability to stay resilient.

After all, Grit Audit is not a self-assessment tool, but a wide-ranging platform for creating a more resilient mindset in en-trepreneurship. Through knowledge and enhancement of their grit, entrepreneurs are in a better position to overcome the challenges that are bound to arise in the process of developing and maintaining a successful business.

Recovery Playbooks

When it comes to entrepreneurship, failures are inevitable as they are educative. It is also essential to design a personal tem-plate that will help to overcome these obstacles, be resilient, and move forward. A Recovery Playbook is a predefined, high-level approach to the obstacles that frequently happen to entrepreneurs. This playbook is not a script, but a flexible plan that gives clarity and direction when fear of the unknown hits.

A Recovery Playbook is simple in its structure. It starts with defining the "Trigger," which is the exact situation or circum-stance that marks the possibility of a setback. The awareness of this trigger will enable an immediate, decisive action known as the Immediate Response. This preliminary step is essential so that the situation does not get out of control. With a prede-termined answer, entrepreneurs are able to reduce panic and take action.

The playbook recommends a time of Reflection after the initial response. It is a stage of learning the reasons and possible consequences of the failure. Questions of a retrospective na-ture, such as What went wrong? And what might have been amended? Assistance in drawing lessons which are essential in avoiding future occurrences of the same problems. The reflec-tion phase is not the one that is concerned with blaming, but rather the one that is concerned with learning and growth.

The last element of the playbook is the Next Step. This entails having a clear action plan to take. It may be the arrangement of a team meeting to discuss the problem or a reshuffling of a project schedule. It is about positive action that drives the ven-ture out of the setback.

There are sample playbooks that can be designed for different cases. To give an example, the Product Flop Recovery play-book may specify actions to be performed in the first 24 hours following the unsuccessful release of a product. This may involve reviewing customer feedback, speaking with the team, and switching the product strategy. On the same note, the Team Conflict Resolution playbook could help an entre-preneur navigate the process of reestablishing a team follow-ing a project failure with a primary focus on communication and collaboration.

It is important to customize such playbooks. Checklists and scenario prompts are used to encourage entrepreneurs to cus-tomize their playbooks to the specifics of their situations. An example may be who to call when you are in trouble or what healthful habit to fall back on when you lose. Cues like a Post-it note summary or a computer reminder can be used to re-mind users of these playbooks in real-time, so that they do not remain simply a theoretical tool but help during the heat of the moment.

Recovery Playbooks creation is a proactive measure for resili-ency development. Also, when entrepreneurs predict disap-pointments and prepare, they can use these as learning and growth opportunities. Such an organized method will, in case of difficulties, make it possible to address the challenges with confidence and clarity and strengthen the entrepreneur's ability to maneuver the intricate environment of business, with grace and foresight.

Using Fail Logs

The principle of failure logs changes the perspective of the entrepreneurs on the use and perception of failures. Instead of taking failures as discouraging information, the use of the fail logs can be a productive way of capturing and celebrating the learning experience in every failure. These journals are literally living documents, and they record the daily or weekly struggles and, more importantly, the lessons that are learned out of every experience.

In its essence, fail logs are made to turn the conversation about failure. They prompt entrepreneurs to group their fail-ures based on their type and severity: it could be an execution error, a misreading in the market, teamwork dynamics, or ex-ternal influences, but doing so will enable them to identify recurring patterns and problems in systems. This classification is not only to be organized but is also a diagnostic tool to learn the underlying causes of the recurrent challenges. Through methodical analysis of such logs, an entrepreneur is able to notice the trends that might not have been realized, thus giving a better understanding of what areas need to be taken into consideration in terms of strategy or a shift.

The habit of keeping a fail log is also concerned with acknowl-edging and glorifying productive failures. These are failures that, though they have a short-term negative effect, are part of long-term growth and learning. The more positive and resili-ent attitude of entrepreneurs can be attained by concentrating on the progress of the failures and not on the mistakes them-selves. Every fail log entry is a marker of advancement--a tes-timony to learning and acclimatization that are superior com-ponents of the entrepreneurial achievement.

Reflections on these logs, which are monthly and called Failure Wins, are chances to note one important thing you have learned in each entry. The ritual not only boosts the im-portance of learning from failure but also fosters an atmos-phere of receptiveness and constant betterment. By communi-cating these thoughts to accountability partners or mastermind groups, the effect can be increased. These collaborative reflec-tions help create a community of learning, in which members of the community can use the experiences of others to make their lives more resilient and creative.

In addition, fail logs are not only personal tools but may also be sent to peers to learn together. This sharing may be done in different forms, e.g., a mastermind Slack channel, in which the snippets of the fail logs are discussed. This will promote positive group introspection regarding the common failures that allow for the breaking of the isolation that tends to follow entrepreneurial difficulties.

Essentially, more than failure recording is involved in the prac-tice of using fail logs. It is concerning how to establish an organized learning and development system. Entrepreneurs would be able to develop the attitude of taking challenges as stepping stones to success by turning them into a chance to gain knowledge. Fail logs, in turn, are a crucial part of the en-trepreneurial toolset that cultivates the culture of tenacity and the ability to adapt constantly. By doing so, entrepreneurs are not only able to go through their paths more knowledgeably but also establish a strong base on which they can continue their growth and innovations.

Restoring Energy and Focus

Energy and focus tend to be ignored, but they are essential aspects in the stressful world of entrepreneurship. A typical enemy is burnout, which is an emotional, physical, and mental fatigue resulting from long-term stress. It presents itself in a specific way to entrepreneurs, and it tends to creep up in be-tween the fray of innovation and development. Early recogni-tion of the symptoms is crucial; they may be constant fatigue, lack of engagement with the business, and lowered productivi-ty.

In order to fight this, structured rituals would be useful in re-storing energy fast and providing long-term well-being. The 90-Minute Reset is one of these rituals, a special plan that gives a chance to take a proper rest and rejuvenate the imagination. This is a matter of creating some time on an intensive work-load and then a considerable rest, where the mind gets re-freshed and gets back to work with renewed energy. This pro-cess can be further improved with the addition of mindful transitional practices, like short, actionable breathwork or movement activities that create a psychological recharge be-tween activities.

The digital detox is another needed practice. In our digital age of constant distraction by devices, it is urgently necessary to reclaim our mental bandwidth. By setting up off time like a promise of having No-Work Sundays, sacred times are formed where mental and emotional renewal can occur. These boundaries must be essential, especially at high-growth stages, because the urges to stay constantly connected are the hardest.

Look at the example of a founder who managed to overcome burnout through the prohibition of email evenings. This basic but powerful boundary was a kind of personal time, and this resulted in more productivity and satisfaction in working hours. It is a boon to the strength of conscious disconnection.

To maintain these practices, it is best to develop a personal plan, a "Burnout Prevention Plan along the way. This plan ought to be dynamic with realistic elements that meet the indi-vidual needs. It could involve the recognition of any threat, the instant reactions, and the individual restoration rites. As an example, when we, instead of checking emails at the end of the day, engage in a creative hobby, we can turn downtime into a renewing experience, and in the process, we become more relaxed and more inspired.

In addition, capitalizing on the strength of the community can increase resilience. Telling accountability partners or master-mind groups about their experiences and strategies is more than support; it leads to learning together. These networks will be able to provide new views and ways out, and convert fail-ures into opportunities for development.

Finally, the energy and focus restoration is connected with developing a sustainable rhythm between work and personal well-being. It involves self-knowledge, restraint, and readiness to spend more of one's time on health rather than being ob-sessively ambitious. With these strategies, entrepreneurs will be able to cope with the challenges of the journey they are going through in a clear and resilient way; thus, they can not only be effective but also fulfilled in their line of action.

CHAPTER 9

BEYOND THE STARTUP

Applying Entrepreneurial Thinking in Any Career

Entrepreneurial thinking goes beyond the conventional limits of beginning a business and can be a potent instrument in any job. This attitude entails creativity, problem-solving, and value creation in spite of the work role. It consists of the ability to see opportunities in the obstacles of other people and imple-ment innovative solutions to effect change and improvement. To individuals who operate in an established organization, assuming the role of an entrepreneur may result in immense personal and professional development.

Intrapreneurs are people in large organizations who utilize entrepreneurial thinking to bring forth innovation within the organization. These people do not begin a new company, but rather they initiate a new process or product inside the com-pany based on the same principles that make successful entre-preneurs. They spot inefficiencies and sell their ideas as inter-nal startups. This will not only create a culture of innovation but also create more job satisfaction since people will feel a sense of ownership and influence.

Entrepreneurial thinking is also transformative in the public sector. By implementing the principles of entrepreneurship, the public sector innovators are seeking methods of enhanc-ing services and addressing complicated issues that affect soci-ety. As an illustration, a leader working with a non-profit or-ganization may employ the concept of minimum viable prod-uct (MVP) to create new programs and ensure that resources are not wasted, and the programs must address the needs of the population.

This is also the attitude being adopted by educators and health care professionals. Educators are creating new curricula and modes of teaching that can address the needs of various learners, and the medical practitioners are also inventing new processes of patient care to enable better results. The profes-sionals are not beginning new businesses; instead, they are changing and adding value to their areas.

In order to successfully employ entrepreneurial thinking in any profession, people can apply numerous tools and models. The Opportunity Radar worksheet is one such tool that assists practitioners in identifying areas of inefficiency and suggesting remedies. Such a proactive strategy motivates them to con-stantly look for challenges that can be growth and improve-ment opportunities.

Entrepreneurial ideas should be implemented through buy-in by colleagues and the leadership. Engaging in influence and recruitment is a process where it becomes necessary to show the worthiness of the idea and get people to side with the cause. Such procedures can be facilitated with the help of scripts and checklists, as they would offer a consistent system to present new initiatives and recruit early adopters within the organization.

With the fast changes in technology and markets, one must keep up with the changing times by being flexible in his/her thinking in order to accommodate new trends and other tech-nological changes. This entails active learning, trend spotting, and up-skilling. The practice of periodically testing new tools and platforms, including generative AI or remote collaboration tools, keeps people on the leading edge of innovation. Inte-grating rites of renewing assumptions and seeking alternative points of view can also help an individual gain a better capacity to adjust and succeed in a new environment.

Finally, entrepreneurial thinking in any profession also enables one to be a transformer and a problem-solver, enabling them to create change and be innovative within their job. This atti-tude not only promotes individual development but also leads to the success and development of the organization in general.

Adapting Your Mindset for New Technologies

With the fast-changing environment of technology, a flexible and adaptable attitude is not only advantageous but is also necessary. The world is experiencing new technological ad-vances that have never before been witnessed, and these are changing industries and redefining the manner in which busi-nesses are conducted. Being an entrepreneur, one must always be ahead of the curve, and that means taking the initiative to learn and adapt.

Technological change is rapid, and anyone who does not keep up with it is at risk of going out of business. This does not simply concern new skills but the development of an attitude that views change as an opportunity and not a threat. One of the main elements of this attitude is the readiness to learn and learn not to be aware. This includes keeping up with the latest in technology and trends by being constantly exposed to in-dustry reports, industry newsletters, and podcasts. The latest developments in your area of activity can be noticed at all times, once the habit of a Trend Tracker is introduced into your routine.

Besides keeping up, it is important to remain experimental with new technologies. This can be done by a new tool chal-lenge, in which you vow to use and evaluate a new online product or service monthly. This is not only a way of boosting your technical expertise but also makes your mind receptive to new-fangled solutions that can be implemented in your busi-ness. As an example, a pilot project based on generative AI or remote collaboration tools could be established to get valuable insights and pave the way for larger-scale applications.

It is also necessary to update your assumptions regularly and find other points of view so that you can avoid being biased successfully. Carrying out a quarterly blind spot audit, in which you seek the input of your peers or mentors as to what you might have missed, can help keep you on your toes and avoid getting stuck in old ways of thinking. It is an effective practice to promote a more holistic perspective, and diverse insights and experiences will inform all your strategies.

Additionally, there must be a quick upskilling system in order to adopt new technologies. This entails the establishment of rituals that reinforce lifelong learning and flexibility. Interaction with the international human resources and communities can be a source of knowledge and assistance. These interactions can make a tremendous contribution to your knowledge and use of new technologies, whether it is attending online forums, participating in webinars, or joining professional networks.

Lastly, the need to remain pertinent in the environment of emerging technologies is not an individual task. The develop-ment of a group of similarly minded individuals who are also determined to be innovative can be mutually supportive and encouraging. Such a network may act as a sounding board for new ideas and a stimulus in tough periods.

To sum up, the process of opening your mind and accepting new technologies is dynamic and continuous. It demands a lifetime learning commitment, willingness to change, and the willingness to adopt new instruments and concepts. By devel-oping these habits and mindsets, you get yourself in a position of not just surviving in the ever-evolving technological world but also prospering.

Building Momentum

Tapping the energy of the inertia is tantamount to taking over the kinetic energy of a rolling boulder. It starts with the tiniest of stimuli, a first shove that sets the whole in motion. This is the first step that is important to overcome the inertia that keeps many entrepreneurs at bay. The difficulty, once set in motion, turns to sustainment and acceleration, so that instead of decelerating, it increases on itself and becomes a powerful force.

The momentum does not always involve speed or force, as people involved in entrepreneurship are often convinced. It is about consistency and direction. Setting up the habit of taking little tiny steps can add up to great strides in the long run. Here is where the strength of micro-goals comes in. The establish-ment of short-term, attainable goals will allow entrepreneurs to take successive steps. These wins are vital because they act as an indicator of progress, and every single one of them makes the belief that the final goal is achievable.

Monitoring is a necessary activity during this process. A basic log or an electronic dashboard would be a device that the en-trepreneurs would use to track their successes and failures. This is a graphical display of progress and is useful in finding patterns, bottlenecks, and celebrating progress. It gives com-pletion and a physical reminder of the progress made, which is especially encouraging in hard moments.

Reflecting is an important point in keeping the momentum. These meetings must concentrate on what is working, what needs to be changed, and where more effort may be needed. Reflective practice not only helps keep the course but also improves strategies to be more in line with the changing na-ture of the entrepreneurial process.

The other pillar of keeping the momentum is accountability. Communicating the goals and progress with someone or a mastermind group provides a support system that motivates you to keep on. These networks provide a platform to get feedback, advice, and encouragement, and turn the otherwise lonely entrepreneurship experience into a cooperative one. Regularly using this network serves as a reminder to the entre-preneurs of their promises, and the mutual sense of responsi-bility acts as a source of motivation.

In addition, it is important to overcome the urge to plan too much or overthink. A roadmap can be described as a simpli-fied version of a roadmap that dwells upon the main mile-stones and metrics. This brief roadmap averts the deconta-giousness of analysis and enables faster decision-making and flexibility. It makes entrepreneurs flexible and prepared to make a pivot or repeat on the basis of real-time feedback and various alterations.

Resilience is a very important aspect in creating momentum. It is the capacity to overcome disappointments and move on that distinguishes between successes and failures. Experience and reflection are the keys to building resilience, as well as learning to fail and make that failure a stepping stone instead of a stumbling block.

Finally, to gain momentum, one has to plan, work hard, and be flexible. It is the building of a chain reaction and a cycle of thinking. This process will drive an entrepreneur to achieve his/her objectives, where one step leads to another and the process becomes a process of success and development. Once the ball starts rolling, confidence and ability will increase, and it will be a self-progressive process of development and achievement.

Overcoming Overplanning

The over-planning habit is a dangerous barrier to prompt action and creativity in the ever-changing entrepreneurship environment. Entrepreneurs can be caught in the snare of planning and perfecting, where the need to execute a plan is lost in the need to perfect the plan. This is what is referred to as overplanning, and it may result in stagnation because one gets into the cycle of preparation without making any pro-gress.

In response, it is necessary to develop a learner approach in planning. The introduction of a one-page startup roadmap is a potent antidote to overplanning stasis. This is the simplified roadmap that serves to compress the spirit of a business plan into a simplified format that emphasizes key aspects, like vi-sion, milestones, metrics, and assumptions. By making the plan not more than a one-page document, the entrepreneurs are made to stay on track and simple, thus making the process of decision-making and implementation faster.

The key to this strategy is focusing on establishing specific milestones and laying down kill criteria, which are set mile-stones at which a project is reconsidered depending on its advancement or failure. This approach makes entrepreneurs seek fast iterations and pivots where needed, instead of being caught in lengthy planning processes. The capability to shift or cancel the project, in case it does not reach the targeted mile-stones, allows efficient use of the resources and aligns the focus on the opportunities that can be followed.

A realistic case study of the practice can be considered in the tale of a corporate worker who managed to start a SaaS appli-cation through a one-page scheme. The professional had to act quickly from the concept to the execution, which involved cutting the complexities of a traditional business plan, proving the effectiveness of the simplified planning process in practice.

Moreover, the one-page roadmap fosters an environment of action over analysis. Entrepreneurs can learn to appreciate progress and flexibility by focusing on what can be done ra-ther than on what can be studied. Such a change of thinking fosters the ability to accept uncertainty as an inherent part of the entrepreneurial process and to become resilient and inno-vative.

When creating a one-page roadmap, entrepreneurs are taken through the process of defining and describing their vision clearly, establishing manageable milestones that align with the long-term objectives, and defining measures of success. Not only does this process make the planning process easier, but it also contributes to the improvement of strategic thinking by concentrating on the most important business development areas.

Finally, to get beyond overplanning, there must be a funda-mental change in planning perception and execution. Through the minimalist attitude towards planning, the entrepreneurs are enabled to be bold, flexible, and creative. A one-page startup roadmap is an essential resource in this transformation, as the culture of action and flexibility is fundamental to success in the rapidly changing world of entrepreneurship.

CHAPTER 10

BUILDING YOUR SUPPORT NETWORK

The Micro-Mastermind Model

In the field of entrepreneurship, the support network cannot be underestimated. Micro-mastermind group becomes an essential tool aimed at the exploitation of collective accounta-bility and idea exchange. These intimate groups, unlike the massive mastermind events or big networking events, offer a more focused approach in which small groups of entrepre-neurs will be able to flourish. These groups are characterized by the fact that they can create increased accountability among each other, exchange ideas, and provide emotional support, which is essential at different stages of the entrepreneurial path.

The micro-mastermind model starts with the choice of a small community or group of peers or colleagues, usually two to four people. This small size will guarantee that every member is able to take direct part in the process and receive individual feedback and encouragement. This is done through a wise choice of the members forming such a group because of complementary skills, where there is a similarity in the goals of the members, making the overall effectiveness of the group good.

After being assembled, the group functions within sense-making meetings in a time-conscious manner. The agenda in these meetings is usually minimalistic and involves sharing recent victories, attending to the existing roadblocks, and mak-ing promises for the next period. The format allows free dis-cussion and gives members a secure platform to share trou-bles and consult. Rituals, including hot seat rotations (mem-bers of the group receive focused feedback) and idea jams (members of the group brainstorm solutions together), are part of keeping engagement and promoting creativity.

To maintain the momentum of the group in the long run, planning and dedication are required. Plans to deal with possi-ble dropouts or time setbacks are fundamental to continuity. The use of the rotating facilitator system may assist in sharing the leadership duties and making the group dynamic and par-ticipatory. Also, setting up a group charter or a ground rules document may help clear up expectations and ensure that eve-ry member agrees with their goals.

The micro-mastermind model also stresses the need to trou-bleshoot to maintain engagement and value extraction. Grace-fully handling dropouts, scheduling conflicts, a rotating system of facilitators, etc., are some of the techniques that can be used to keep the group alive. An example of such a foundational document can be a group charter or ground rules document, making sure that every member is on the same page in his or her commitments and expectations.

The micro-mastermind model helps entrepreneurs to have access to an effective support network that not only keeps them accountable but also motivates and challenges them to take things to new levels. Through mutual experiences and understanding, these groups are able to develop a culture that allows those with entrepreneurial intellect to thrive, create, and endure through common experiences and insights. The mi-cro-mastermind group is therefore a testament to the effec-tiveness of collaboration within an entrepreneurial world and provides a different kind of support, accountability, and crea-tive synergy.

Finding Allies in Unlikely Places

The skill of finding and capitalizing on allies in unforeseen places can be quite a potent resource in the complicated and sometimes lonely path of entrepreneurship. These friends, within the non-traditional networks, can offer priceless sup-port, insights, and opportunities that otherwise may not be utilized. It is important to broaden the definition of a network because it has a wider range than the traditional business or professional groups. It encompasses alum networks, neigh-borhood associations, and hobby clubs, as well as coworking areas, where each has a distinct perspective and resources.

The nature of this strategy is the acknowledgment of the pow-er of neglected relationships. Numerous entrepreneurs have found key partners, advisors, or early consumers in settings that are much further away than normal startup ecosystems. As an example, I would like to mention the case of a founder who, trying to reinvent the image of her brand, has collaborat-ed with a local artist whom she met during a community art lesson. This partnership would not only continue to add an impressive visual identity to her brand but also access a new audience in the form of artistic circles.

The other strong illustration is the case of an entrepreneur who discovered a pool of beta users within a cycling club at a local park. The first group, which was contacted as a personal interest, was very helpful in giving crucial feedback and word-of-mouth recommendations, which were hugely helpful in the iterative development of the product. These examples high-light the need to look at each social interaction as a way of doing business.

In order to make any use of them, it is necessary to map and activate these hidden networks. This entails a methodical pro-cess of finding and interacting with contacts that may not be such allies at first glance. One helpful resource in this journey is called the Hidden Network Worksheet, wherein the business owner is advised to add friends, family, former classmates, and service providers to the list because they could be con-nected to a sector of interest or an area of knowledge. The question that appears the easiest to answer is, Who do you know that knows someone in your target industry? It may play the role of a catalyst to come up with these latent networks.

The way to approach these non-industry contacts is to be confident yet tactful. These interactions can be enabled by the use of outreach scripts and confidence boosters that make awkward situations productive conversations. Templates of emails and texts, as well as conversation starters that are spe-cific to unlikely allies, will facilitate the reconnection with dormant contacts or the initiation of conversations with new acquaintances.

As one grows their support system, it is also worthwhile to be receptive to the various types of support these allies are willing to provide, which could be mentorship, partnership, or cus-tomer insight. The lives of entrepreneurs who have ever man-aged to move through these non-traditional networks are tes-timonies of how much broader the net should be thrown. Entrepreneurs may find a rich pool of opportunities and sup-port networks by going out of their comfort zones and ex-panding their social networks, which contribute to their busi-nesses in unintended ways.

Handling Naysayers

Doubt and skepticism are two inseparable friends in the en-trepreneurial process. They are present in all directions, be it family, friends, or the market itself, and such experiences shape the resolution and vision of any new entrepreneur. It is not just an obstacle but a transition that most, possibly every-body, entrepreneurs will have to go through. Having realized what this criticism is all about and, more to the point, how to make the most of it, one can turn perceived negativity into a potent source of development.

The first way of dealing with naysayers is by realizing that criticism is not necessarily done with ill intent or intent to harm, but may be based on a pure concern or lack of understanding. It is a psychological reaction to the uncertainty that business start-ups have. This is demonstrated by a short story of a reader who was doubted by others when starting his business. Although the first step can be a sting, this kind of feedback can be a mirror and help identify areas that could use addi-tional focus or enhancement.

Entrepreneurs can use mental models and reframing strategies in order to manage criticism effectively. These strategies aim to filter the noise and find some constructive insights to make progress. An example of these methods is known as the feedback filter exercise, and it aids in the separation of valuable advice and noise. By classifying feedback into types and set-tling on the most appropriate response plan, the entrepreneur will be in a position to take criticism with a clear and strategic mind.

An example is actionable scripts that can be used to respond to negative feedback professionally. Even a simple response to an offhand remark on LinkedIn or a thank-you note email can defuse awkwardness and create opportunities for a productive conversation. These scripts are used as a means of keeping the cool and getting the dialogue on more fruitful paths.

In addition, emotion-processing of the emotional conse-quences of criticism rituals is essential. Such rituals help to regain confidence and guarantee forward movement. Such questions as What's the kernel of truth in this feedback? are used as a reflection. Promote self-reflection, and make busi-ness people learn to apply substantial wisdom to even negative feedback. Criticism can also be beneficial by sharing with a peer group, which will put the criticism in perspective and turn it into an opportunity to improve a product or service.

Resilience of the entrepreneur is evidenced by the skill to re-frame criticism. It is all about looking at every bit of feedback as an opportunity to update and improve, and not a failure. With an embedded habit of providing feedback to other trust-ed peers, entrepreneurs are able to obtain useful insights that otherwise may not be obvious. This cooperative strategy builds the strength of the individual as well as a nurturing community that lives on collective wisdom.

The key to dealing with naysayers is, ultimately, a balance be-tween listening and filtering, openness to outside views, and determination to stay on track to one's vision. It is about the development of a strong skin, not to close the world off, but to experience it better. As business people learn how to cope with these stormy waters, they not only strengthen their busi-nesses but themselves, coming out stronger and better in-formed than they were.

Building Community Online

The internet presents an expansive and dynamic field where businesspeople can develop and interact with the communi-ties. It is a virtual community that is a hotbed of networking like-minded people around the world through platforms like Slack, Indie Hackers, and LinkedIn. These platforms can ena-ble the entrepreneur to not only build his or her networks but also to create a depth of interaction that is not limited by the axiomatic geographical barriers.

The entry point to navigate these communities is to find out who is part of which group and which channel is relevant to the entrepreneurial interest and objectives. The entrepreneurs are advised to find niche-based communities that may connect with their particular industry or business model because the communities tend to offer specialized information and re-sources. After identification, the process of entering such communities is not simply a kind of participation; it is about an active approach to the process.

The first measures include the development of an intelligent introduction that predetermines further communication. An effective opening post can be a source of discussion, encour-aging other people to present their experiences and thoughts. It is advisable to describe the existing difficulties and solicit feedback in this introduction, as well as establish a sense of cooperation and mutual support.

Involvement in these online communities is also enhanced by attending activities like Ask Me Anything (AMA) sessions, feedback threads, and virtual events. Such interactions not only increase visibility but also create credibility in the community. These activities will prove to be valuable since they will show dedication and give great chances to offer and receive support.

We can connect more, and a sense of belonging can be built through weekly rituals like sharing personal wins or finding accountability partners. These rituals become the points of contact that strengthen the purpose of the community and may result in creating permanent professional relationships. It is also always good for entrepreneurs to offer assistance or even share resources since this tendency of being generous usually results in a mutual move, increasing the network.

A digital tracking network that monitors and maintains these relationships may prove to be a treasure trove. This system of organization assists in monitoring the interactions and making follow-up reminders to ensure that not a single connection is left. The ability to have a record of engagements allows the entrepreneur to develop his or her network strategically so that informal interactions may be converted to strong professional networks.

The challenges to establishing an effective community on the internet are not so mundane. It must be consistent, active, and desire to see others grow. Nevertheless, the advantages of a well-bridged and active Internet community are innumerable. It offers a layer of support, inspiration, and a place of innovation and teamwork.

Essentially, the concept of using online communities is one in which the entrepreneur can flourish by creating a symbiotic environment. It is about turning virtual space into a living eco-system of growth, where ideas are shared, support is provid-ed, and success is shared. Not only does this digital camarade-rie boost personal endeavors, but it is also adding to a culture of creativity and cooperation, becoming a global culture of innovation and collaboration.

CHAPTER 11

LEADERSHIP IN ACTION

Navigating Difficult Team Moments

It is unavoidable to encounter challenges in a team in the dynamic environment of entrepreneurial ventures. Such are the times when tension and uncertainty may prevail, and the bal-ance between leadership and empathy is due. Such situations need to be handled with a set of different strategies aimed at facilitating communication, restoring trust, and steering the team through the storm.

Active and empathetic listening is the basis of overcoming tough team situations. This includes ensuring that a team works in an environment that makes each member feel heard and understood, even in times of heightened emotions. It is essential to take into consideration individual opinions, and one should give people the opportunity to voice their worries without being judged. This is not only a way of cooling things down, but also of discovering the problems that are underly-ing the conflict.

After clearing the air, the emphasis is directed at the collabora-tive framing of the problem. By allowing the team to perceive the problem as a group problem and not a performance fail-ure, one will have changed the dynamic to one of collabora-tion as opposed to conflict. This view promotes a feeling of togetherness and collective responsibility and encourages the members of a team to collaborate and find a solution.

Communication is the most important thing at such times. Leaders should have a clear and succinct story that defines the status quo, the desired position, and actions to take to close the gap. This story is also an eye-opener; it reminds the team to be on track even when there is a lot of confusion. Being transparent on risks and possible hurdles is also critical be-cause honesty and credibility are earned.

Rushing decisions in the heinous hour is also a tendency that may come up in order to mitigate the pain. Nevertheless, it is important to take time to stop and think. This time off gives time to study the situation more thoroughly, making it possible to make informed decisions. The leaders are supposed to foster a Pause, Acknowledge, Align approach whereby they all pause to help them evaluate the situation, consider the emo-tions and opinions of each member of the team, and agree on a course of action.

Regaining trust once a fight has occurred is a slow process that must be exercised as time goes on. An open channel of communication and frequent check-ins can be useful in repair-ing any divisions. These relations must be provided in a way that facilitates transparency and accountability and upholds the desire of the team to continue on the journey. Also, it is pos-sible to celebrate little successes along the way to the goal, which will restore the spirit of the team and support the posi-tive behavior.

Vulnerability cannot be overemphasized in leadership during tough times. Leaders set a growth mindset by sharing their own experiences and recognizing their own mistakes, which shows that failures are just learning opportunities. Such vulner-ability builds a culture of transparency and resilience that pro-motes the ability of team members to take risks and not be afraid of failure.

The art of dealing with challenging team situations entails em-pathy, thought, and communication. Leaders can use their collaboration, transparency, and the creation of an enabling environment to turn these problems into opportunities to grow and innovate. The result is that these trials can only strengthen the teams, make them more cohesive, and enable them to face future challenges better.

Feedback as Fuel

Feedback is not merely a mechanism for evaluation; it is a vital component of growth and improvement within entrepreneuri-al teams. Reimagining feedback as a continuous and empower-ing tool rather than a periodic critique becomes a catalyst for development and innovation. This transformation starts with embedding feedback. Feedback is not just an evaluation in-strument, but it is an important part of development and en-hancement in the entrepreneurial teams.

It transforms feed-back into a development- and innovation-driving power by redefining it as an ongoing and enabling force instead of one that is performed periodically and serves as a critique. This process begins with the incorporation of feedback within the organizational culture and therefore becomes an intrinsic as-pect in all interactions and decision-making within the organi-zation.

The process of building the culture of feedback starts with creating routine, systematic feedback opportunities among the team members. This may be conducted as Feedback Fridays or open office hours during which team members can bring up issues and successes openly. Through these practices, the feedback becomes normalized, and the stigma surrounding feedback is dissolved to make the process more open and productive.

Feedback has to be practical and actionable. Such a format as the Stop/Start/Continue feedback approach can be intro-duced to provide brief, pointed interactions that emphasize what has to be stopped, what has to be started, and what has to be continued. This approach will see feedback being fo-cused and closely related to action items, hence it will make it easier for individuals and teams to implement changes and improvements.

Honest and fruitful feedback processes cannot happen with-out psychological safety. Teams are supposed to develop clear rules of engagement that help to foster respect and openness, such that all members are not afraid to contribute their ideas and thoughts without the fear of being judged or retaliated against. These regulations act as a guideline in the development of trust and transparency, which are fundamental to establish-ing a favorable feedback atmosphere.

Feedback may, however, sometimes give rise to defensive responses or sound ambiguous and useless. In order to over-come these obstacles, it should be noted that the advice on troubleshooting should be provided so that the general feed-back can be converted into clear steps that can be implement-ed. The mitigation of defensive reactions can also be done by promoting a mentality that perceives feedback as a learning experience instead of an assault on the individual.

As a practical solution, digital tools that enable peer reviews and constant improvement can be used to complement feed-back rituals. The feedback process could be made less cum-bersome and efficient with the help of tools such as Google Forms or Slack integrations. Such instruments can be used to gather and process feedback immediately, which is a good source of information that can be used to make tactical deci-sions and build the team.

Finally, feedback must be considered as an active and continu-ous process of entrepreneurship. Through the creation of a culture that supports feedback as a driving instrument of de-velopment, teams can unleash the power of feedback to stoke innovation, enhance performance, and succeed. The feedback may become a potent source of personal and organizational development, and even the basic evaluation means can be developed into a heavy engine with the help of practice and proper structures.

Diversity as a Competitive Edge

In the current fast-changing business environment, diversity is not just a buzzword- it is a key generator of innovation and competitive advantage. Organizations that have diversity within their workforce can exploit a pool of ideas, experiences, and competencies that contribute to creativity and problem-solving. This subsequently results in the creation of products and services that can appeal to more customers and markets.

Varied teams pool together diverse individuals of different backgrounds, including different cultures, genders, ages, and experiences. This combination of views will enable the organi-zation to have a better view of the global markets since the team members will be able to give an insight into consumer behaviors and preferences that would not otherwise have been identified. The companies can more effectively serve and fulfill the needs of their customers by reflecting the diversity of the marketplace within their own ranks, thus developing customer loyalty and engagement.

Moreover, diversity fosters resilience. A diverse team is more flexible in a world that is ever-changing and where the unfore-seen may bring down even the best-laid plans. The varied experiences and viewpoints within such a team encourage flexible thinking and innovative solutions to challenges. This flexibility is essential to new businesses and old businesses alike to get them through tricky situations and to grab oppor-tunities that other businesses miss.

Companies should not just be satisfied with the idea of repre-sentation since it is necessary to be inclusive in order to lever-age the full potential of diversity. This involves the ability to make an environment where everyone has a voice that is re-spected and where members of the team are empowered to play their part to the fullest. Inclusive practices, where everyone has a platform to voice his or her insights and ideas, are pos-sible through inclusive activities, including idea sharing on a round-robin basis or anonymous suggestion tools. Such prac-tices not only improve decision-making but also inspire a sense of belonging and commitment among the team mem-bers and may result in increased retention rates and job satis-faction.

The effect that diversity has on performance is well docu-mented. Research has indicated that organizations that have diversified leadership stand a higher chance of performing better than others in terms of profitability and productivity. The fact that diversity is positively correlated with enhanced company performance is evidence of the effect that diverse points of view can have on strategic planning and implemen-tation.

Nonetheless, a diverse and inclusive workplace can only be realized through deliberate and hard work. Business organiza-tions should be able to take strategic steps that lead to the recruitment, retention, and development of talent in un-derrepresented groups. This may involve outreach initiatives to communities in general, mentoring, and job descriptions that attract a variety of candidates. Moreover, organizations are also encouraged to engage in continuous training to make everyone realize the importance of diversity and learn skills to work in diverse teams.

Mini-case stories of effective diverse teams provide a display of the transformative energy of diversity. An example is of a multinational remote product team exploiting the merits of the different cultural backgrounds of its members to develop a product that could attract a global market. On the same note, a startup can change its business model due to the input of a non-traditional team member, which results in breakthrough outputs.

In a nutshell, diversity is a strong competitive advantage that can spur innovation, strength, and market insight. Because they integrate diversity and inclusion into the operating system, companies achieve not only better performance, but also make the business world more fair and dynamic.

Meeting Makeovers

A change of the conventional meeting format to a more dy-namic, experiment-based format can have a huge impact on increasing productivity and innovation within a team. Rather than a traditional model, when meetings usually turn into a status update, this model promotes sessions that focus on quick experimentation and real outcomes. With a change to an "experiment-first" structure, every agenda item is directly asso-ciated with a hypothesis or a test. This change motivates peo-ple working in the team to become more immersed in the material and create an atmosphere where ideas are being checked and improved on the fly.

The first step of the experiment-first approach is to redesign the meeting agenda. Each item should explain the idea intend-ed to be tested, the criteria of success, and the actionable steps. The clarity not only brings the team on the same track but also preconditions productive discussions and decision-making. An example of such a weekly product sync is having every team member present a recent experiment, what was being tested, its results, and the lessons. This is the practice that will promote accountability, as well as promote a culture of contin-uous improvement and learning.

Facilitation is very instrumental in making these meetings pro-ductive and inclusive. Facilitation tips are to switch the facilita-tor role in order to avoid bias and promote new ideas. More-over, it is possible to incorporate those tools as silent brain-storming and the digital use of whiteboarding to come up with ideas without the pressure of verbal feedback. These tools could be used to make the environment more inclusive, and everyone on the team could share their thoughts and ideas.

Post-meeting protocols are needed in order to make sure that the experiments talked about in meetings result in what can be acted on. Action checklists and follow-up strategies are also embedded to aid in the tracking of the experiments and in the lessons learned. The next steps and responsibilities to be per-formed by each team member can be recorded in an action tracker template, e.g. Additionally, digitalization obtained through such tools as a Slack reminder bot can help keep the team informed on the progress of the experiment and on potential changes.

The shift of meetings towards experiment-based meetings not only helps to increase the level of engagement but also leads towards innovation, as it fosters an attitude that is inclined towards testing and learning. This will assist in silo busting in the team and create a collaborative environment where ideas can be shared and refined freely. The redefinition of the pur-pose and structure of meetings can help teams transform the process of sharing updates into an active process of experi-menting and learning, which will help them ensure their faster growth and success in a competitive environment.

CHAPTER 12

EMBRACING FAILURE AS A LEARNING TOOL

Fail Fast Ritual

The philosophy of fail fast becomes central in the changing world of entrepreneurship. It does not concern irresponsible risk-taking but a calculated learning and adjusting. Such an attitude makes entrepreneurs feel comfortable failing as an essential part of the innovation work and use it as an experi-ence that can be learnt. The core of this philosophy consists of the fact that it allows differentiating between failing fast and failing carelessly, and the significance of structured reflection and progressive improvement.

Fundamentally, the idea of the fail-fast approach is to speed up the feedback loop. Entrepreneurs are encouraged to test soon, collect information, and adjust or persist on the basis of field evidence. This approach saves time that is wasted in dead ends and improves the capacity to find considerate strategies within a short period of time. Through the establishment of a repeat, low-friction personal debrief system, people can empir-ically break down what worked, what didn't, and what to at-tempt next. It is not a process about focusing on the failures, but using them as a stepping stone towards success.

Developing a personal debrief system is one of the basic points of this ritual. It is a systematic contemplation of all the activities or experiments, irrespective of whether they paid off. Entrepreneurs are advised to utilize such tools as the Fail Fast Debrief template, which allows answering such important questions: What went right? What went wrong? What can be improved? Such templates work as a guide, showing the way future work should proceed and making sure that every failure contributes to an expanding body of knowledge and experi-ence.

Another component is the sharing of debriefs with peers or accountability partners. This habitualizes failures, making it a culture of not stigmatizing failure, but it is a necessary element of the entrepreneurship process. Through the Failure Share circles, entrepreneurs can get other perspectives and experi-ence from others, and brainstorm solutions together. This collective strategy is not only able to support the learning pro-cess of each person but also the entrepreneurial ecosystem.

Failure data helps improve future performance, a very im-portant skill in the contemporary entrepreneur. The results of this transformative power are demonstrated in the real-life examples. Take the example of a side project that first failed, but over time, with several iterations and failure data, turned into a successful project. These tales are examples of how the philosophy of fail fast can convert short-term failures into long-term triumph.

These habits should be integrated into everyday life to develop resilience and flexibility, which are the key characteristics of surviving in the unstable world of entrepreneurship. Entrepre-neurs are advised to start every day by writing a pre-mortem journal to envision possible obstacles and brainstorm solu-tions. Reflections after failure further cement the learning, and in this way, every experience is used to further growth and development.

Finally, the ritual of "fail fast is also about developing an atti-tude that looks at failure as some data, which can be used on the way to innovation. It motivates business people to make risky decisions that are calculated, learn fast, and be nimble. This philosophy will help people to survive the chaotic world of entrepreneurship with a sense of confidence and clarity, and make any failure their stepping stone into success.

Learning from Setbacks

Failures are integral to the entrepreneurial journey, yet they are often perceived as the end of the road rather than the means. Entrepreneurship is fraught with failures, and they are seen as the conclusion and not the means. In order to become a genuine success, it is imperative to have a new definition of setbacks. These are tough moments, but the lessons that ac-company them are invaluable and can be used to achieve suc-cess in the future. Viewing failures as learning experiences will allow the entrepreneur to become more of a growth experi-ence than a frustrating one.

There is a lesson, a secret benefit, in every failure, which must be discovered. Rather than perceiving failures as mistakes they are making, entrepreneurs ought to take them as a chance to acquire information and improve their plans. This change of thought is essential. It enables people to be emotionally dis-connected from the setback and think of it in a problem-solving manner. Examination of what went wrong, the reason, and how to prevent it in the future makes a setback a potent learning instrument.

In order to minimise setbacks, it is important to note what happened and what effect it has had. It will entail taking a plunge into that situation, asking probing questions such as what could have been done differently. And what were the outer influences that entered into this? These realizations may expose the latent problems that would otherwise not be no-ticed. This process not only helps to figure out the present setback, but also prevents the same from happening in the future.

Another major element of setback learning is to build resili-ence. Resilience is not only about bouncing back but also about making a better reservoir of strength and wisdom to do it. Entrepreneurs can develop resilience through having a flex-ible mindset, being open to new information, and being ready to change their strategies. It is this flexibility that enables them to turn around when faced with challenges effectively.

Besides, failure has the potential to drive creativity. Restrictions tend to be a creative element that pushes business people to think beyond the box and devise innovative solutions. The new thinking is capable of giving rise to breakthroughs that would otherwise not have been available without the setback that it brought about. It is the adage that need is the mother of invention.

One of the ways in which a practical approach to learning through setbacks can be accomplished is by establishing a setback story bank. It is a compilation of experiences that rec-ord failures, lessons learnt, and remedial actions taken. Main-taining such a record has several functions: it reminds one of the learning experiences gained in the past, gives hope in diffi-cult moments, and can be an invaluable source of help when advising someone with less experience.

Also, an entrepreneur can be equipped with a recovery play-book to help during periods of failure. This playbook must detail possible obstacles and the responses to obstacles that were pre-planned. A series of actions prepared can ease stress and guarantee a faster healing process in case of setbacks.

To conclude, one should accept failures instead of being afraid of them. They belong to the world of entrepreneurs, and giv-en the right attitude, can cause more success. Thinking of fail-ures as a chance to learn and develop, entrepreneurs can over-come the challenges on their way and use possible obstacles as stepping stones. Such an attitude not only prepares them to face future challenges but also gives them the tools necessary to succeed in the highly dynamic world of entrepreneurship.

Building Resilience

Resilience is one of the key qualities in the world of entrepreneurship, and it is one of the cornerstones of entrepreneurial achievement. This virtue, which can be defined as the skill to recover after a blow, is not an inborn trait but a deliberate skill that can be developed with the help of practice and a change of mindset. Fundamentally, resilience is concerned with staying through the challenges and failures that come along with the entrepreneurial path, turning them into chances to learn and grow.

The entrepreneur's life is full of uncertainties and challenges, and one must have the mindset where failure is a stepping stone but not a stumbling block. In order to develop resili-ence, one should be able to recognize the worth of failure first. Every failure is a lesson in itself, a lesson to improve methods and tactics. With a "fail fast" mindset, the entrepreneur is able to cycle through their ideas, learn, and change direction. This will not only hasten the learning process but also reduce the emotional weight of failure so that recovery and progress can be made much faster.

One feasible way of building resiliency is the creation of a "Recovery Playbook. This instrument is a pre-decided flowchart in case of a frequent business failure. Not knowing what to ex-pect next, entrepreneurs can lessen the effect of sudden-onset problems by planning. The playbook contains certain triggers that lead to the immediate response, as well as thoughts and strategies for the next steps. Such an organized practice will guarantee that failures will be managed methodologically, and one will not experience the risk of being overwhelmed by emotions, but will develop an active attitude.

In addition, the idea of the Failing Log can also prove signifi-cant in the process of creating resilience. By recording failures and the new knowledge obtained through them, entrepreneurs can trace the tendencies, see which aspects should be im-proved, and celebrate productive failures that will lead to a general improvement. This habit is not only the standardiza-tion of failure, but also the development of transparency and lifelong learning. Their benefits could be increased by sharing these logs with a supportive community, where peers will pro-vide feedback and insights, which would otherwise go unno-ticed.

Besides personal habits, a positive network can be very im-portant in the development of resilience. Forming a micro-mastermind and/or creating a Resilience Circle can offer the emotional and strategic resources to get through the difficult periods. These groups provide an avenue of sharing experi-ences, brainstorming to find solutions, and holding each other accountable for growth and progress. The wisdom and sup-port gained in such groups can actually help a business person in a great way to endure and survive in times of trouble.

In conclusion, the concept of developing resilience is con-cerned with the attitude toward challenges that view them as something that cannot be tackled by the end of the day, but as a chance to innovate and improve oneself. It entails the devel-opment of habits and structures that ensure unending devel-opment, a sense of optimism and realism, and the ability to use failures as a driving force to a better place. People can not only endure the harshness of the entrepreneurial process but also come out as better and more competent people who are able to accomplish their long-term objectives by instilling the element of resilience within their entrepreneurial experience.

Turning Failures into Opportunities

Failures are viewed as inevitable tragedies that may put a stop to the process of entrepreneurship and demoralize the spirit. However, the capacity to convert such failures into opportuni-ties is a characteristic feature of a resilient entrepreneurial mind. It starts with the basic change of thinking- to see failure as an important learning experience on the journey to success. This attitude involves business owners developing a proactive atti-tude according to which any failure is dissectible to provide insights and lessons.

In order to utilize the power of failures, entrepreneurs have to be receptive and curious about them first. This entails accept-ing the emotional influence of failure and, at the same time, seeking the causative factors. This way, the entrepreneur is able to recognize patterns, systemic problems, or external elements that led to the hiccup. This reflective practice benefits not only personal development but also gives the entrepreneur more problem-solving skills, which would help them tackle future challenges with better acumen.

One of the practical methods to transform failures into op-portunities is the application of guided debriefing, or Failure Debriefs as they are often called. Such meetings make entre-preneurs openly evaluate what has gone wrong, what could have been done otherwise, and what new tactics can be pre-sented in the future. These debriefs are never about making mistakes but also about building up a culture of constant im-provement and innovation. They are used as an open discus-sion board where team members can give different perspec-tives, thereby diversifying the learning process.

Furthermore, the failures can be taken by the entrepreneur as a starting point for pivoting. Pivoting is the strategic change of the business model or the product offering due to the knowledge obtained in the case of a failure. This is not a change of the initial vision but an improvement of the vision to align it with the market requirements and demands. An in-depth insight into customer feedback, market trends, and the competitive market has defined effective pivots. When busi-ness owners know how to pivot, they are also good at evaluat-ing the signs of change and responding promptly to stay rele-vant and/or achieve growth.

The second crucial thing about the transformation of failures into opportunities is the development of resilience and grit. Resilience helps an entrepreneur to survive the emotional ef-fects of failure and continue to pursue long-term goals. Grit, however, contributes to the process of perseverance required to make it through the tough road of entrepreneurship. Col-lectively, these aspects enable entrepreneurs to consider failures as short-term challenges and not as unsurpassable ones.

The second practical way of transforming failures into oppor-tunities is through creating a helpful network of mentors, col-leagues, and advisors. These people are able to give advice, support, and alternative perspectives, where the business peo-ple are able to look past the setbacks and look at newer op-portunities. By being part of a group of similarly minded peo-ple, one develops a feeling of belonging and has a sense of purpose, which may be invaluable when it comes to difficult times.

Finally, turning failure into an opportunity is a skill that can be developed over time. It involves a readiness to risk, accept the unpredictable, and see every failure as a stepping stone to higher achievements. This attitude will open new horizons of innovation, development, and achievement, and the so-called roadblock will be transformed into a strong stepping stone toward new undertakings.

CHAPTER 13

STAYING RELEVANT

Adapting to New Trends

The capability to change in accordance with new trends is not merely an advantage in the fast-changing environment of business, but it is also a requirement. Entrepreneurship is a dynamic world due to changes in technology, market needs and requirements, and consumer expectations. The mindset that entrepreneurs need to develop should be flexible and proactive so that they are able to see something before it hap-pens instead of just responding to it.

The technological innovation is a very fast process, and the number of new tools and platforms is growing every minute. Successful entrepreneurs are those who recognize the need to be lifelong learners and constantly keep track of the newest trends. This will involve forming the habit of listening to in-dustry-specific content regularly through newsletters, podcasts, and reports so as to be updated on new technologies and market changes. Entrepreneurs can stay ahead of the pack and identify opportunities before they are mainstream by making it part of their everyday routine.

The other important thing about the adjustment to new trends is experimentation. Entrepreneurs ought to create an ambiance that would promote the use of new tools and approaches. They can use pilot projects to test the usefulness of new tech-nologies in a low-risk environment. As an example, the explo-ration of generative AI or a remote collaboration tool could be of great use in understanding how it could be used and what value it could offer to a business environment. This modality not only encourages innovation but also reduces the dangers involved in taking unproven technologies.

In addition, entrepreneurs should frequently question entre-preneurial assumptions. The business world is in a continuous flux, and the same methods that might have been effective yesterday might not be effective today. A practical method of keeping one's business strategies up to date is by holding quarterly blind spot audits, where peers or mentors are con-sulted to point out the areas that may be missed with regard to opportunities and threats. Such a cycle of finding different points of view can give opportunities that were unknown be-fore and make the entrepreneurs correct their strategies ac-cording to the latest trends.

The international character of the present market dictates the wider outlook. Entrepreneurs should always be receptive to global ideas and innovations. Experiencing the world and its resources may bring discoveries and inspiration. This could be through attending international forums, or global entrepre-neurship networks, or just updating the trends of the world market.

Finally, the skill of accommodating new trends is accompanied by a desire to learn constantly and be open to the transfor-mations. Entrepreneurs should be ready to abandon out-of-date habits and work with new concepts that contribute to the development. Such an attitude not only helps in overcoming the complications of the contemporary business environment but also sets entrepreneurs on the path to success in the con-stantly evolving world. With these practices implanted in their daily operations, the entrepreneurs would be able to keep their businesses afloat, proactive, and able to withstand the uncer-tain tides of change.

Proactive Learning

In a world where the rate of technological change and market forces is unremittingly accelerating, the proactive learning atti-tude is the key to success for any individual who wants to succeed in the world of entrepreneurship. Such a strategy in-cludes constant engagement towards the learning of new skills and knowledge, predicting changes in the industry, and re-maining at the forefront as opposed to responding to altera-tions.

In order to develop this mentality, one will first need to admit the intrinsic dangers of complacency. The business sphere is full of instances of the formerly dominating companies that could not succeed due to their inability to predict technological changes or market shifts. This raises the need to come up with a system of continuous learning and trend spots. Habits that people or companies should practice on a regular basis are to use Trend

Trackers (by subscribing to industry-related news-letters, listening to industry podcasts, reading market reports, etc.). Such practices put entrepreneurs in a position where they understand that the changes are coming and how to adjust their strategies to respond to them instead of being surprised.

In addition, proactive learning is not limited to passive information consumption. It entails actively exploring new tools and platforms so as to improve the skill set. One of the sensi-ble ones is the monthly new tool challenge in which people pledge to test out and review a new digital tool or service. These initiatives will not only build familiarity with new tech-nologies but will also allow creative problem-solving through promoting experimentation in low-stakes settings.

The other core element of proactive learning is the conscious update of assumptions and the search for different points of view. Entrepreneurs ought to conduct a regular blind spot audit, in which they consult with peers or a mentor and identi-fy any potential opportunities or threats that they had ignored. This practice plays a vital role in being able to see the entire picture of the business world and to make sure that the strate-gies one has are not outdated and are efficient in their execu-tion.

Moreover, it is crucial to have a global mentality. In the con-temporary globalised world, learning does not take place local-ly. Entrepreneurs must also actively find international re-sources and communities to have information about different markets and different cultures. This international outlook will be able to reveal new possibilities and encourage new solutions that would not be evident in a local perspective.

Lastly, it would be imperative to create rituals that help to sus-tain a proactive mindset by encouraging lifelong learning. Planning periodic reflection and self-review sessions, e.g., quarterly, helps you not know your own blind spot, assists in recognizing areas of development, and establishes new learn-ing objectives. Also, being a part of international communities and forums may be a source of useful feedback, as well as encouragement to create a culture of constant learning and change.

To conclude, there should be no such thing as passive learn-ing, as it is an essential part of entrepreneurial success. The entrepreneur will be in a position not just to survive but also to flourish in the constantly changing business environment by being knowledgeable, trying new things, and allowing different ways of thinking. It is this dedication to learning and change that can, in the end, distinguish the successful and the stagnant so that entrepreneurs can create resilient and progressive busi-ness organizations.

Trendspotting

In this contemporary dynamic business environment, identifi-cation and exploitation of new trends are not merely an art but a requirement for all entrepreneurs. The increasing pace of technology, changing consumer preferences, and markets that are volatile and dynamic require an active trend-spotting strate-gy. Identifying trends, even before they enter the mainstream, can give an advantage and lead to new possibilities.

One of the initial steps in trendspotting is developing a habit of lifelong learning. This involves subscribing to a diverse information feed, including industry reports, podcasts, and newsletters. Frequent interaction with different and credible sources can aid in the development of an overall process of understanding the market environment. By creating the habit of checking these sources once a week, the entrepreneurs are able to keep up with all the recent news and the possible shift in the industry.

Being willing to put in place and use new technologies is an-other necessary component of trendspotting. The corporate world is full of tales of firms that have been caught in the snare of technology upheaval due to their inability to either innovate or adjust accordingly. In order to prevent such a trap, entrepreneurs must push themselves to investigate new tools and platforms on a regular basis. As an example, pilot projects can be installed using new technologies such as generative AI or remote collaboration tools to obtain first-hand experience of the possible effect of these innovations on business pro-cesses.

Further, trendspotting cannot only be concerned with tracking technological progress but also with the change in consumer behavior and preferences. The entrepreneurs should be cus-tomer-centric, pursue feedback, and monitor shifts in con-sumer needs.

This could be in the form of carrying out fre-quent surveys, listening to social media, and analysing custom-er information to find out new trends and preferences. In this way, companies will be in a position to customize their prod-ucts to suit changing consumer demands and to remain com-petitive.

Challenging the current assumptions and finding alternative points of view are also important in closely observing trends. Entrepreneurs should carry out regular blind spot audits. Such audits entail seeking the feedback of their peers, mentors, or even customers to point out areas that could have been missed. Also, a connection with the outside world can offer new knowledge and deepen the understanding of market dy-namics beyond national borders.

Trendspotting is a process that is connected to the spirit of flexibility and perseverance. Complacency is a major threat as the rate of change keeps increasing. Entrepreneurs should be alert and adept at adjusting strategies where required and ac-cept change as a chance and not as a challenge. This proactive thinking mindset allows the possibility of survival and even prosperity of businesses in the face of uncertainty.

Finally, to learn to spot trends, one must also be willing to participate in lifelong education, trial and error, and be ready to receive other opinions. By incorporating these practices into their entrepreneurship experience, one can strategically place oneself in a position to predict and take advantage of emerg-ing trends. It is not only a way of growing the business; it also stimulates innovation and long-term sustainability in a con-stantly evolving world.

Lifelong Learning

Constant learning, constant adaptation is the key in the ever-changing environment of entrepreneurship. Such a lifelong learning process is not limited to the institutional realm but can be applied to all aspects of life, and it is a way of thinking that will survive on curiosity and endurance. In attempting to wade through the intricacies of their business, entrepreneurs need to create a culture of lifelong learning that will enable them to be nimble and progressive.

Lifelong learning is initiated with the desire to be self-aware and identify gaps in his/her knowledge. It is advisable to per-form frequent self-assessments of entrepreneurs in order to determine areas in which they can develop their knowledge and skills. This reflective exercise not only allows one to identi-fy areas of improvement but also creates a culture that appreci-ates promotion rather than perfection.

The volatility of the contemporary business world requires the entrepreneur to keep up with the changes and technologies introduced to the market. This demands a dynamic style of learning whereby one drives him or herself to acquire new knowledge and competencies. With the subscription to indus-try newsletters, webinars, online courses, and so on, it is al-ways necessary that entrepreneurs focus on continuous learn-ing as one of their strategic tools to remain relevant and com-petitive.

Besides, learning is not an isolated process. The interaction with various communities and networks can greatly benefit entrepreneurs. They have access to a richness of knowledge and worldviews by connecting with peers, mentors, and in-dustry experts. Such contacts are the driving force behind innovation because they introduce entrepreneurs to alternative opinions and experiences, which encourage them to think of new solutions and methods.

Learning to take on failure as a learning experience is also part of the practice of lifelong learning. The entrepreneur is en-couraged to look at the failures as milestones to be learnt in-stead of a goal. By evaluating failures and deriving lessons, they can improve their policies and make better decisions. This is the strength in the presence of adversity that is a characteris-tic of successful entrepreneurial attitudes.

Integrating lifelong learning into everyday life may have a number of forms. Entrepreneurs may have special times of studying, pondering, or working on their competencies at one time of the week. They can also have life experiments where they willingly leave their comfort zone to have new hobbies and interests. These experiments not only accelerate individual development but also motivate creativity and innovation in their career fields.

Finally, lifelong learning is the development of a changing and committed mindset. It gives the entrepreneurs the ability to adjust to the dynamic nature of business and to take opportu-nities as they are presented by new knowledge and under-standing. Incorporating this attitude into the day-to-day rou-tine, entrepreneurs not only develop their personal and pro-fessional competencies but also help to promote the wider culture of innovation and progress.

In their lifetime, entrepreneurs make it a characteristic of their journey as they remain in their careers through the lifelong learning process. The reaction is testimony to their commit-ment not just to succeeding but also to developing in a world that never rests. This continuous learning process gives entre-preneurs the strength and flexibility to survive amidst uncer-tainty, so that their businesses have a long-term chance to be successful and meaningful.

CHAPTER 14

CONCLUSION

Summarizing the Journey

Following the complex twists and turns of the entrepreneurial journey, a complex web of experiences that have threads of prestige, perseverance, and change becomes apparent. The quest to learn an entrepreneurial mindset goes further than ambition, and it enters a new world where all challenges are transformed into places of growth and development.

The nature of entrepreneurship is in the unremitting search for innovation and the boldness to follow unexplored paths. This is not a trip within the confines of setting up a business; it is a way of thinking that extends into all life areas and makes peo-ple think on their feet and act decisively. It is regarding the development of a mindset that believes in uncertainty and perceiving failure as a stepping stone to success.

In this journey, there is the learning to tear down restrictive perceptions that tend to be chains of holding potential. The procedure resembles a matter of de-peeling the layers of un-certainty and trepidation, unveiling a backbone of strength and will. It is important to break through these inner obstacles, which will enable them to turn fear into a motivator to act, and they will be driven towards their objectives with fresh energy and acuity.

One of the most critical things in this journey is how to move ideas to action. It entails a methodology of converting abstract ideas into concrete results. This is not restricted to the use of strategic frameworks but also the development of a mindset that will thrive in the practice of experimentation and error. The skill of rapidly shifting and adapting to emerging infor-mation or shifting situations is the attribute of a successful entrepreneur.

The role of resilience in this story is very crucial. It is the foun-dation that sustains the people in their highs and lows in en-trepreneurial ventures, which are inevitable. The concept of resilience is the development of the ability to overcome adver-sity, to learn through errors, and to continue onward in the right direction in spite of obstacles. It entails the development of a positive and realistic attitude, which helps one to make sure decisions even in the face of uncertainty.

In addition, the trip also focuses on the need to work together and create a supportive network. It is imperative to be able to lead and inspire entrepreneurial teams and create an environ-ment in which creativity and innovation may thrive. This is not just the skill of effective communication but also the skill to utilize different opinions and capabilities.

It is also important to create a strong support system. One should surround oneself with mentors, peers, and advisors who offer guidance, feedback, and encouragement, as this can help immensely in the entrepreneurial journey. These networks present a great source of information and provide inspiration and accountability.

At all, the entrepreneurial mind path is a self-discovery/self-development process. It is a lifelong dedication to learning and adapting, being open to new experiences, and incessantly find-ing ways to become better. Such an attitude would result in a proactive attitude toward change, which would make people predict the tendencies and innovate in that way.

When one takes a retrospective look at this journey, it is clear that the ultimate success is not in where one reaches but in the number of improvements one makes during the process. Eve-ry single action, every obstacle to be conquered, and every lesson acquired leaves its strong thread in the rich tapestry of entrepreneurship life, setting the course to future success and personal satisfaction.

Key Takeaways

Knowledge about the entrepreneurial mindset means not only having the theoretical knowledge about the concepts, but also being an active participant in the principles that make success-ful entrepreneurship. One of the most valuable lessons that were learned in the process of learning how to handle this type of mindset is that resiliency and adaptability need to be cultivated. Entrepreneurs have to be ready to take losses and reorient their course of action when they have to. Creating a way out of problems and working against all odds are also characteristic of a good entrepreneur because of his/her ability to stay focused and determined.

The other important lesson is that of lifelong learning and self-evaluation. Entrepreneurs exist in a state of never-ending self-assessment, where they give feedback on their strengths and weaknesses, and constructively use this feedback to im-prove themselves. This self-examination and adjustment not only aid personal development but also remain relevant in a fast-moving business world. Conducting periodic self-evaluations and being receptive to new ideas will keep the en-trepreneur at the forefront of innovation at all times.

In addition, the entrepreneurial path highlights the importance of a good support network. The presence of a good peer group of mentors, peers, and advisors can offer useful in-sights and support, enabling an entrepreneur to go through any tricky situation and make wise decisions. The network is also a source of motivation and accountability. The entrepre-neur is likely to remain focused on his or her goals and main-tain the course despite the hardships involved.

The other significant lesson is how to make choices under uncertainty. Entrepreneurs have to learn to make quality choic-es fast and with much less information. This entails striking the right balance between instinct and data-based analysis to reduce risks even as the potential rewards are maximized. Cre-ation of a powerful decision-making model can assist business people in thinking effectively and making the most suitable decision.

Moreover, the entrepreneurial thinking emphasizes the neces-sity to balance optimism and realism. Though a positive atti-tude and faith in the vision are necessary, it is also necessary to base the expectations on reality. This balance also helps entre-preneurs to make realistic goals and to evade overconfidence traps.

Last, innovation and creativity are the core entrepreneurial success values to embrace. Entrepreneurs are challenged to be innovative, to break the box, and to go beyond the norms to find unusual solutions to issues. This is a creative way of doing business that not only results in unique products and services but also a culture of growth and constant improvement in their businesses.

In short, to be able to master the entrepreneurial mindset, it is a mixture of resilience, continuous learning, good decision-making, and innovative problem-solving. By making them an essential part of themselves, the business people will be able to manoeuvre through the twists and turns in the business world without fear and with constant success.

Celebrating Progress

The milestones made in this journey or the hustle are as essen-tial in the dynamic nature of entrepreneurship as recognizing them. Progress, as an element that is often covered up by the constant drive to achieve the next big thing, has its time in the limelight. These accomplishments not only serve as a motivat-ing factor but also offer a self-reflective time to analyze the progress achieved. This reflection is not a mere pause but a tactical reset, enabling the business people to take a look at the course of action and reevaluate their strategies when it comes to future activities.

Each of these actions, big or small victories, is a part of the bigger story of development. These periods of advancement are not only indicators of success but also signs of the strength and responsiveness to a constantly evolving market. It is through a celebratory approach that entrepreneurs build a feedback mechanism to strengthen positive behavior and mo-tivate them to keep practicing effective behaviors. This celebra-tion is a motivational compass, which helps people navigate the unavoidable trials and pitfalls that accompany the entre-preneurial journey.

The practice of praising improvement is compound. It not only includes the individual accomplishments but also the group accomplishments of a team. Rewarding teamwork builds an appreciation culture and teamwork. The culture is critical towards making a strong team, unified, inspired, and aligned with the organizational vision. This recognition may be seen in a wide variety of forms, including basic recognition in the meeting, official award or recognition, and, as a result, the morale and commitment of the team will be improved.

Further, the celebration of progress is a chance to learn and repeat. Every milestone achieved can also be a very instructive experience in terms of what succeeded, what failed, and why. Such analysis plays a vital role in streamlining the processes and improving efficiencies. Business people with a continuous improvement mindset see success as a stepping-stone to more innovation and improvement. They record these learnings, thereby building a database of knowledge that they can revisit when commencing projects later on, lessening the learning curve and speeding up the process.

Telling stories is also part of celebrating progress in the larger context. It is a process of creating and telling the story of the journey and emphasizing the obstacles and the successes achieved. The story is a strong marketing instrument that can appeal to prospective investors, partners, and customers who can identify with the story of this brand. Through such stories, entrepreneurs are able to create a community around their brand and create loyalty and engagement.

Eventually, the milestone of celebrating progress is being able to embrace the journey as well as its ups and downs. It is a call to remember that not only the final product matters, but also the experiences and development that happen in the process of being an entrepreneur. As they deliberately mark these oc-casions, business people can have a fair look at the distance they have travelled without forgetting where they are heading. This equilibrium is important to maintaining motivation and passion in the long run.

Therefore, the process of rejoicing in the advancement is far more than simply recognizing successful results. It is a strategic behavior that improves motivation, team cooperation, learn-ing, and business storytelling. By so doing, it makes the entre-preneurs ready to take on future challenges with renewed vig-our and confidence, guaranteed growth, and success.

Continued Action

The spirit of long-term development in the sphere of entre-preneurship is the possibility to act constantly on the vision, no matter what challenges appear on the way. This continuous activity is not a process of persistence; it is a process of strate-gic adaptive movement that makes sense in changing goals and conditions. Entrepreneurs are usually subjected to a hurri-cane of issues, which will test their spirit, such as market vola-tility and unforeseen operational hitches. The trick would be to use them as stepping stones and not as stumbling blocks.

The psychological attitude of persistence to act is in proactive decision-making. Entrepreneurs are advised to expect possible challenges and develop adaptable plans that would permit them to make timely turns. This is not only the establishment of clear and attainable goals but also keeping up a dynamic plan that can be adjusted with the appearance of new infor-mation and opportunities. It is about developing resilience in the form of an attitude that perceives change as something that is always there and that setbacks are chances of learning and growth.

Further development of a good support network is a critical element of continued action. Entrepreneurs also flourish in an environment where they feel they are surrounded by mentors, peers, and advisors who can bring various viewpoints and understanding to the table. They act as sounding boards to which an entrepreneur can present ideas, get critical feedback, and encouragement that will drive them. Moreover, the act of associating with a group of other entrepreneurs may result in a collaboration and partnership that presents new growth and innovation opportunities.

Practically, the continued action means the process of dividing the bigger goal into small parts, thereby preventing the sense of being overwhelmed by a huge project at first glance. This step-by-step method not only makes the process more man-ageable but also instills a sequence of small successes that give rise to momentum and confidence. Every task that one does as a finisher is a block, strengthening the dedication of the entrepreneur to his or her vision.

Furthermore, reflection and review are part of long-term ac-tion. Entrepreneurs are advised to review their progress on a regular basis and analyze what approaches have worked and in which aspects changes are possible. This reflection approach assists in streamlining future actions and ensures that they are consistent with the overall goals. It is a process of planning, taking action, reviewing, and making adjustments that enables the business person to stay on course.

Entrepreneurial environment has been described as one where there is a lot of change and uncertainty, thus adaptability is an important element of action continuation. Entrepreneurs are required to be experimental, take wise risks, and learn through successes and failures. This form of experimentation pro-motes innovation, and it enables entrepreneurs to find a new way to succeed that they may not have thought of in the first place.

Finally, persistence is concerned with pushing ahead regardless of the opposition. It needs a combination of will, adaptability, and strategizing. In such a manner, by providing the environ-ment that leads to continual learning and adaptation, entrepre-neurs are able to operate their business ventures and be confi-dent and clear in terms of their complexities. This ruthless drive in the name of progress does not just drive personal achievement but also forms part of the wider horizon of in-novation and economic development. By doing so over time, entrepreneurs not only fulfill his or her own objectives, but also encourage others to follow their dreams with the same passion and commitment.

EPILOGUE

As we reach the end of this exploration into mastering the entrepreneurial mindset, it's essential to reflect on the trans-formative power that lies within the principles shared. This journey has been one of self-discovery, practical learning, and the relentless pursuit of personal and professional fulfillment. Throughout these pages, the idea that entrepreneurship is not merely a career path but a mindset has been a central theme, emphasizing that anyone, irrespective of their starting point, can cultivate this mindset to build a life aligned with their deepest values and aspirations.

The tools and frameworks provided are designed to be adapt-able, encouraging you to take control of your narrative and to craft a life that is uniquely yours. By integrating these strategies into your daily routines, you are equipped to turn challenges into opportunities, fostering resilience and creativity in the face of adversity. Every exercise, from the micro-experiments to the scenario planning, serves as a stepping stone towards greater self-efficacy and confidence.

The stories of diverse entrepreneurs who have navigated set-backs and turned them into growth opportunities serve as a reminder that failure is not the end, but a crucial part of the learning process.

Embracing a culture of experimentation and feedback allows for continual improvement and innovation, making you more adaptable to the changing tides of the mar-ket and technology.

As you move forward, remember the importance of commu-nity and support networks. Whether through mastermind groups, peer accountability partnerships, or mentorship, these connections provide the encouragement and feedback neces-sary to sustain your entrepreneurial spirit. They are the anchors that will keep you grounded and motivated, offering perspec-tives that challenge your assumptions and broaden your hori-zons.

This book is not just a guide but a companion in your ongo-ing journey. It is a resource to revisit whenever you find your-self in need of inspiration or guidance. The entrepreneurial mindset is not a destination but an evolving practice, one that requires ongoing reflection and adaptation. By consistently applying the insights gained from this book, you are not only building a business but crafting a life of purpose, passion, and freedom.

The call to action is simple yet profound: continue to challenge yourself, step into discomfort, and let each small step lead to transformative change. Thank you for allowing these pages to be part of your journey. May you carry forward the lessons learned and continue to create, innovate, and inspire on your terms.

www.ingramcontent.com/pod-product-compliance
Lightning Source LLC
Chambersburg PA
CBHW070932210326
41520CB00021B/6899